HEDDA GABLER; THIS IS NOT A LOVE STORY

by Henrik Ibsen

In a new version by Selma Dimitrijevic
From the literal translation
by Karin and Anne Bamborough

‖SAMUEL FRENCH‖

samuelfrench.co.uk

FOR AMATEUR PRODUCTION ENQUIRIES

UNITED KINGDOM AND WORLD
EXCLUDING NORTH AMERICA
plays@samuelfrench.co.uk
020 7255 4302/01

Each title is subject to availability from Samuel French,
depending upon country of performance.

THINKING ABOUT PERFORMING A SHOW?

There are thousands of plays and musicals available to perform from Samuel French right now, and applying for a licence is easier and more affordable than you might think

From classic plays to brand new musicals, from monologues to epic dramas, there are shows for everyone.

Plays and musicals are protected by copyright law so if you want to perform them, the first thing you'll need is a licence. This simple process helps support the playwright by ensuring they get paid for their work, and means that you'll have the documents you need to stage the show in public.

Not all our shows are available to perform all the time, so it's important to check and apply for a licence before you start rehearsals or commit to doing the show.

LEARN MORE & FIND THOUSANDS OF SHOWS

Browse our full range of plays and musicals and find out more about how to license a show
www.samuelfrench.co.uk/perform

Talk to the friendly experts in our Licensing team for advice on choosing a show, and help with licensing
plays@samuelfrench.co.uk   020 7387 9373

Acting Editions

BORN TO PERFORM

Playscripts designed from the ground up to work the way you do in rehearsal, performance and study

---

Larger, clearer text for easier reading

Wider margins for notes

Performance features such as character and props lists, sound and lighting cues, and more

---

+ CHOOSE A SIZE AND STYLE TO SUIT YOU

  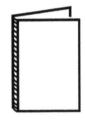

STANDARD EDITION	**SPIRAL-BOUND EDITION**	**LARGE EDITION**
Our regular paperback book at our regular size	The same size as the Standard Edition, but with a sturdy, easy-to-fold, easy-to-hold spiral-bound spine	A4 size and spiral bound, with larger text and a blank page for notes opposite every page of text. Perfect for technical and directing use

LEARN MORE | **samuelfrench.co.uk/actingeditions**

Other plays by SELMA DIMITRIJEVIC
published and licensed by Samuel French

Gods Are Fallen And All Safety Gone

A Prayer

FIND PERFECT PLAYS TO PERFORM AT
www.samuelfrench.co.uk/perform

ABOUT THE AUTHOR

Selma is Greyscale Theatre Company's Artistic Director.

Theatre credits include: *Dr. Frankenstein* (Greyscale/Northern Stage); *A Prayer* (Greyscale/NorthernStage); *Night Time* (Traverse Theatre); *Broken* (Oran Mor); *Game Theory* (ek/ Traverse Theatre); *Re:Union* (7:84); *Harmless Creatures* (Greyscale/ Hull Truck); *Gods Are Fallen And All Safety Gone* (Greyscale/Almeida); *The Gamblers* (Dundee Rep/Greyscale).

Translations include: Theatre – *Otto and Jonah* (Robert Holman); *Knives in Hens* (David Harrower); *Enda Walsh* (Bedbound); *Blackbird* (David Harrower); *The Gamblers* (Gogol); *The Two of Us* (Tena Stivicic).

Fiction – *Ground Beneath Her Feet* (Salman Rushdie); *The Snapper* (Roddy Doyle); *White Teeth* (Zadie Smith); *Brick Lane* (Monica Ali); *The Autograph Man* (Zadie Smith); *How Late It Was How Late* (James Kelman); *Porno* (Irwin Welsh); *Night People* (Barry Gifford); *A Heartbreaking Work Of Staggering Genious* (Dave Eggers).

AUTHOR'S NOTE

In September 2016 I spent a week in Oslo, at the Ibsen Festival, watching versions, adaptations and interpretations of Ibsen's plays. At the same time, I was writing my own new version of *Hedda Gabler*, with the subtitle, "This Is Not A Love Story". I don't know where the subtitle came from or why I decided to give Hedda the last word – but I knew I was not interested in trying to discover or explain who Hedda really is, but rather in giving her the opportunity to do that.

Hedda Gabler has been described as sociopath, unhappy, beautiful, destructive, petty, funny, trivial, profound and of course – so very bored. My starting point was that she herself doesn't know what or who she is and that is why she is so desperately unhappy in a context that is – if compared to lives of many other women around the world – not catastrophic.

Without changing the text I wanted to allow Hedda an opportunity to pause. To stop for a moment, take a deep breath and look at the world around her. Really look at it.

At the beginning of the play, there is a flicker, time stops for just a second or two. Then, as Hedda observes others, people who seem to know what they want and need, time stops for a bit longer, and Hedda learns it stops for everyone else but not for her. Finally, as the play goes on, she learns how to stop the time herself, how to pause life when she needs to. She learns how to buy herself a few precious moments in order to see the world for what it really is. In it's final moments, this power allows her to reject the versions of her life presented to her as her only options – either to live as subject to the cruel will of others or to kill herself. She chooses to say no to both, to shed the life she lives and to walk into the future, slamming the door behind her just as Nora did.

This is not supposed to be the definitive version, or even a version "better" or "more faithful" than the others. It is just one of the many ways to look at the fascinating person that is Henrik Ibsen's *Hedda Gabler*.

Selma Dimitrijevic, 2017

A Northern Stage and Greyscale co-production

Henrik Ibsen
Hedda Gabler; This Is Not A Love Story

In a new version by Selma Dimitrijevic
From the literal translation by Anne and Karin Bamborough

First performed at Northern Stage, Newcastle-Upon-Tyne on
16th February – 8th March 2017

CAST

HEDDA GABLER	Victoria Elliott
TESMAN	Ed Gaughan
LOVBORG	Scott Turnbull
THEA	Rachel Denning
AUNT JULIE	Libby Davison
JUDGE BRACK	Donald McBride
BERTE	Polly Frame

CREATIVE TEAM

Director	Selma Dimitrijevic
Artistic Collaborator	Lorne Campbell
Set & Costume Designer	Tom Piper
Lighting Designer	Lizzie Powell
Sound Designer & Composer	Scott Twynholm
Assistant Director	Victoria Copeland
RTYDS/Greyscale Young Director Placement	Rebekah Bowsher
BSL Interpreter	Faye Alvi

STAGE MANAGEMENT

Company Manager	Colin Holman
Stage Manager	Lee Davis
Deputy Stage Manager	Nichola Jayne Reilly
Assistant Stage Manager	Nicola Morris

Northern Stage

Northern Stage, Newcastle upon Tyne, makes ambitious, intelligent, enjoyable theatre. We have a reputation for reviving classic plays in fresh adaptations and creating bold new work.

We have been one of the UK's most popular national touring companies for the last 20 years. Alongside our own work, we present the best local, national and international theatre. Our extensive Creative Residencies programme supports local and national theatre-makers to develop their work at Northern Stage and our year-round programme of projects and events encourage people of all ages and backgrounds to take part in making theatre.

Greyscale is an international theatre company based in Newcastle.

Through a programme of reimagined classics and bold new writing we bring together artists and audiences interested in conversations about the contemporary world.

We co-produce with large and small venues across the UK and our work has been seen at The Gate, Almeida, Northern Stage, Theatre Royal Bath, Hull Truck, Royal Exchange Manchester, Traverse, Tron, Dundee Rep as well as at international festivals.

Greyscale is proud to be an UNLIMITED ALLY; celebrating the work of disabled artists as part of the Unlimited programme.

Greyscale associate company for 2016 – 17 is GOBSCURE, led by writer and theatremaker sean burn.

CAST

Victoria Elliott – Hedda Gabler

Theatre credits include: *The Season Ticket; Get Carter, Cat on a Hot Tin Roof, Oh What a Lovely War, Wind in the Willows, Hansel and Gretel, Pub Quiz* (Northern Stage), *I Can't Sing!* (West End), *Tyne, 13.1, Jump, Me and Cilla, A Nightingale Sang, Rhino and the Drum, Lush Life* (Live Theatre), *Two, As You Like It* (Manchester Royal Exchange), *Cooking With Elvis* (Hull Truck).

TV credits include: *Boy Meets Girl, The Kennedys, Hebburn, Truckers, The Ministry of Curious Stuff, Holby City, 55 Degrees North* (BBC), *Emmerdale* (ITV), *Steel River Blues* (Granada).

Ed Gaughan –Tesman

Ed Gaughan is a writer, actor, comedian, director and musician.

In 2010, with double-act partner Andrew Buckley, Ed starred in and helped script long-time collaborator Nick Whitfield's feature film *Skeletons*, which was nominated for a BAFTA, a BIFA and won The Michael Powell Award for Cinema at Edinburgh International Film Festival. Ed was then nominated for The Peter Sellers Award for Comedy in 2011.

Buckley and Gaughan have written and performed shows at Edinburgh Festival, Soho Theatre, Lyric Hammersmith, BAC and Manchester Royal Exchange. Ed is a member of the award-winning group The London Snorkelling Team, and, along with Will Adamsdale, has co-written and performed with the LST at Edinburgh Festival (winning a Herald Angel), Camden Roundhouse, Latitude and opened for Portishead at Alexandra Palace.

Ed co-writes, (along with Adamsdale, Buckley and the LST) performs and curates Night of Stuff at Shoreditch Town Hall, a 21st-century vaudeville showcasing the finest in comedy, music and strange performance. He has acted across stage, screen and radio. He was nominated for Best Actor at the MTAs for Sean Holmes production of *A Midsummer Night's Dream* in 2013. He is much in demand as an extremely versatile voice actor, most recently appearing in the BBC's reboot of *Dangermouse* voicing many characters including DM's iconic arch-enemy Baron Von Greenback. He has worked as a director and comic consultant for top UK comics such as Josie Long and Milton Jones, sketch teams such as Pappy's and leading physical comedy company Spymonkey. Ed trained as a jazz musician for many years and has composed soundtracks for many shows including Nabokov's award winning *Symphony*.

Scott Turnbull – Lovborg

Scott's theatre credits include: *Where Do All The Dead Pigeons Go?* (Northern Stage/Greyscale); *Gods Are Fallen And All Safety Gone* (Greyscale); *Get Santa* (Northern Stage); *The Rubber Room* (The Old Vic); *The Machine Gunners* (Polka Theatre); *Apples* (Northern Stage); *The Tempest* (KG Productions); *Book of Beasts* (Catherine Wheels Theatre Company); *Hansel and Gretel* (Northern Stage); *Heartbreak Soup* (Empty Space Productions); *A Christmas Carol* (Northern Stage) and *How Many Miles to Basra?* (The West Yorkshire Playhouse).

His television credits include: *Little Bastard, Wolfblood, The Royal Today, The Bill* and *Byker Grove*. He was chosen by *The Independent* as 'One to Watch' in 2011 and was awarded North-East Actor of the Year by The Journal, 2010.

Rachel Denning – Thea

Rachel trained at Mountview Academy of Theatre Arts.

Her theatre credits include: *See How They Run* (Reduced Height Theatre Company), *The Government Inspector* (Birmingham Rep), *The Vote* (Donmar Warehouse).

Television credits include: *Life's Too Short* (BBC/HBO), *The Vote* (more4), *Call The Midwife* (BBC/Neal St Productions).

Rachel is also a trained Youth Worker and has worked with young people and drama in a variety of settings.

Libby Davidson – Aunt Julie

Libby has worked extensively in the North East at Live Theatre and Northern Stage amongst many others.

She has numerous television credits and radio experience, including: *The Bill, Byker Grove, Our Friends in The North, Holby City, Purely Belter, Doctors* and *The Royal Today*. Recently she has also been working as an educational support worker for a little girl with Down's Syndrome in a local primary school.

Donald McBride – Judge Brack

Donald hails from Fencehouses, County Durham, where he is known by his proper name, Donald Reed. He began working at Live Theatre Newcastle in 1977 and appeared in the first -ever production of *A Nightingale Sang* by C.P. Taylor. Three years with Orchard Theatre in Devon gave him the opportunity to play a one-man show, *Bold Squire Arscott*, about one of the last men in England to keep a professional jester, Black John the Tetcott Merry Man. Donald has played extensively in rep and on tour, including a season with the RSC in Stratford and London, two more one-man shows, *Joe Lives On (The Life of Joe Wilson)*, and *Choir* by Lee Mattinson.

Extensive radio work has included: *My Uncle Freddie* and *The Little World of Don Camillo* and he has appeared in odds and ends of television from time to time. Aside from theatre work he is a keen genealogist and has traced one family line back to 1690.

Polly Frame – Berte

Polly's theatre credits include: *Henry V* (Regent's Park); *The Odyssey: Missing Presumed Dead* (Everyman, Globe and tour), *The death of King Arthur* (Globe), *Mermaid* (Shared Experience), *Sir Gawain and the Green Knight*, (Globe) *Arcadia* (Bristol Tobacco Factory).

After Miss Julie (young Vic), *Earthquakes in London* (Headlong/ The National) *Macbeth* (Chichester, West End, Broadway), *66 Books* (The Bush), *Twelfth Night*, (Filter/RSC)

Cleansed (Oxford Stage Company).

Polly has worked as a director on *We Don't Live Here Anymore*, (Reading Arts and The New Wolsey) and is a creative associate for the performance company Bodies in Flight.

TV includes: *Silent Witness, The Tunnel, Man Down, Meet the Magoons, Servants, Bunny Town, The Accused, Casualty, Holby City, Eastenders, Doctors, The Hope Diamond.*

Film includes: *Macbeth, Half Light* and *Duplicity*.

CREATIVE

Selma Dimitrijevic – Director

Selma is a director and writer and artistic director of Greyscale. Previous directing credits include *Waterproof* (Oran Mor), *Cyrano de Bergerac* (Oran Mor), *Incident At The Border* (Oran Mor), *What Would Judas Do?* (Greyscale/Almeida/Hull Truck), *A Prayer* (Greyscale/Northern Stage), *Tonight David Ireland Will Lecture Dance And Box* (Greyscale/Northern Stage), *Gods Are Fallen And All Safety Gone* (Greyscale), *A Beginning, A Middle and An End* (Greyscale/Stellar Quines), *Dead To Me* (Gary Kitching and Co.) and *The Gamblers* (Dundee Rep/ Greyscale).

Selma's plays have been performed in the UK, Germany, Georgia, Canada, Russia, Ukraine and Croatia, and include new versions of Gogol's *The Gamblers* (Dundee Rep) and a new version of *Dr Frankenstein* (Northern Stage/Greyscale).

www.greyscale.org.uk

Lorne Campbell – Artistic Collaborator

Lorne trained at Liverpool John Moores University, The Royal Conservatoire of Scotland and on the Regional Theatre Young Director's Scheme. He is the Artistic Director of Northern Stage and formerly has been: the co-founding Artistic Director of Greyscale; Associate Director of the Traverse Theatre; Creative Fellow of the RSC and Warwick University; Course leader of the BA Directing programme at Drama Centre London.

Credits include: *Get Carter* (Northern Stage), *The Bloody Great Border Balled Project* (Northern Stage), *Get Santa* (Northern Stage), *Cyrano De Bergerac* (Northern Stage), *Tenet* (Greyscale/ Gate), *Tonight Sandy Grierson Will Lecture Dance and Box* (Greyscale), *A Prayer* (Greyscale) *Cherry Blossom* (Traverse Theatre/Teatri Polski, Bydgosczc), *Distracted* (Traverse Theatre), *Brokenville* (British Council/Ensemble of Tolgiatti) *The Nest* (Traverse).

Tom Piper – Set & Costume Designer

Current and future projects include: *The Seven Acts of Mercy* (RSC); *Pelléas et Mélisande* (Garsington Opera).

Theatre designs include: *The Intelligent Homosexual's Guide to Capitalism and Socialism With a Key to Scriptures* (Hampstead Theatre); *Harrogate* (HighTide & Royal Court); *Pride and Prejudice* (Regent's Park Open Air Theatre & UK Tour); *A Midsummer Night's Dream* (RSC & UK Tour); *Carmen la Cubana* (Le Chatelet, Paris); *Endgame, Hamlet, The Libertine, King Lear* (Citizens Theatre, Glasgow); *Red Velvet* (West End, Tricycle Theatre and New York); *A Wolf in Snakeskin Shoes, The House That Will Not Stand* (Tricycle Theatre); *The King's Speech* (Birmingham Rep, Chichester Festival Theatre and UK Tour); *Mermaid* (Shared Experience); *Tamburlaine The Great* (Theatre For a New Audience, New York); *Bakersfield Mist* (West End); *The Big Meal* (Theatre Royal Bath & Hightide Festival); *Bracken Moor* (Shared Experience and Tricycle Theatre); *Zorro* (West End, Tour, Paris, Moscow, Amsterdam, Tokyo and Atlanta); *Goodbye To All That, Vera, Vera, Vera* (Royal Court Theatre and Theatre Local); *Richard III, The Tempest* and *As You Like*

It (Bridge Project at BAM and the Old Vic); *Dealer's Choice* (Menier Chocolate Factory and West End); *Fall* (RSC at the Traverse); *Spyski* (Lyric Hammersmith and tour); *The Scarecrow And His Servant* (Southwark Playhouse); *The Plough And The Stars, The Crucible* and *Six Characters in Search of an Author* (Abbey, Dublin).

Costume designs include: *Pride and Prejudice* and *A Winter's Tale* (Regents Park Open Air Theatre).

Tom was the Associate Designer of the RSC for ten years. His recent work there includes *Love for Love, Christmas Truce, Anthony and Cleopatra* in a new edit by Tarell Alvin McCraney (RSC/Miami/New York), *Boris Godunov, Much Ado About Nothing, Macbeth* and *City*.

MADAM, the Histories Cycle (Courtyard Theatre and at the Roundhouse), designing *Richard II, Henry IV – parts 1 and 2, Henry V, Henry VI – parts 1, 2 and 3* and *Richard III* for which he won the 2009 Olivier Award for Best Costume Design and was nominated for the 2009 Olivier Award for Best Set Design, *As You Like It, The Grain Store, The Drunks, Hamlet, King Lear, The Tempest.*

Opera includes: *Orfeo* (Royal Opera House and Roundhouse); *Eugene Onegin* (Garsington Opera); *Falstaff, Macbeth* (Scottish Opera).

Elsewhere Tom has worked at the NT, the Donmar, the Royal Opera House, Soho Theatre, Dundee Rep, Bush Theatre, Gate Dublin, Nottingham Playhouse, Royal Court Theatre, Hampstead Theatre, Sheffield Crucible and in the West End.

Installations/exhibitions include: *Dr Blighty* (Nutkhut, 14-18 NOW); *Blood Swept Land And Seas of Red* (Tower of London 2014, and UK Tour, 2015 – 2018, with artist Paul Cummins, and in collaboration with Alan Farlie Architects); *Curtain Up* (V&A and Lincoln Centre New York, 2016); *Blood* (Jewish Museum, 2015-2016); *Staging The World* (Shakespeare Exhibition as part of the Cultural Olympiad, British Museum, 2012).

Tom received an MBE for services to theatre and First World War commemorations in 2015. *Blood Swept Lands And Seas of Red* has won numerous awards, including, amongst others, a Museum and Heritage award and a Southbank Sky Arts award; and with Paul Cummins, he was named The Telegraph's Briton of the Year 2014. A series of installations featuring the two sculptural pieces from the installation, designed by Tom, are on tour around the UK until 2018.

Lizzie Powell – Lighting Designer

Theatre credits include: *The Mountaintop* (Young Vic); *Glasgow Girls* (National Theatre of Scotland/UK Tour); *Our Ladies of Perpetual Succour* (National Theatre of Scotland/UK Tour); *Human Animals* (Royal Court); *Hansel & Gretel, Endgame, The Choir, Fever Dream: Southside, The Libertine, Far Away/ Seagulls, Krapp's Last Tape/Footfalls* (Citizens); *The Brink* (Orange Tree); *Violence and Son* (Royal Court); *Fruit Trilogy* (West Yorkshire Playhouse): *Romeo and Juliet* (Sheffield Crucible); *Anna Karenina* (Royal Exchange, Manchester/West Yorkshire Playhouse); *Secret Theatr*e (Lyric, Hammersmith/ Tour); *In A Time O' Strife, My Shrinking Life, The Enquirer, An Appointment with the Wickerman, Knives in Hens, Girl X, Transform Glasgow, Mary Queen of Scots Got Her Head Chopped Off, Our Teacher's a Troll, Rupture, Venus as a Boy* (National Theatre of Scotland); *White Gold* (Iron Oxide); *Idomeneus* (Gate); *Cinderella, Mother Goose, Jack and the Beanstalk* (Perth); *Caged, Poppy and Dingan, The Book of Beasts* (Catherine Wheels); *Spring Awakening, While You Lie, Any Given Day, The Dark Things* (Traverse); *Pangaa* (Ankur); *Huxley's Lab* (Grid Iron/Lung Ha's/Edinburgh Festival Theatre); *Under Milk Wood* (Theatre Royal, Northampton); *The Death of Harry Leon, Making History* (Ouroborous, Dublin); *Cockroach, The Dogstone/Nasty, Brutish and Short, Nobody Will Ever Forgive Us* (National Theatre of Scotland/Traverse).

Scott Twynholm – Sound Designer and Composer

Scott Twynholm is a musician and composer based in Glasgow.

Recent dance and theatre productions include: *Purposeless Movements* (Birds of Paradise), *Denton and Me* (EFF 2016), *Love Struck* (BalletLORENT), *The Gamblers* (Greyscale/Dundee Rep), *Wallace* (National Theatre/The Arches), *Catch-22* (Northern Stage), *Endurance* (A Moment's Peace), *Far Away* (Citizens Theatre), *If these Spasms Could Speak* (The Arches), *Good with People* (Paines Plough) and *Girl X* (NTS).

His compositions have appeared in numerous films including: Palme d'Or nominated *The Edukators* and Cameron Crow's *Vanilla Sky*. Recent film work includes feature documentaries: *Alasdair Gray – A Life in Progress* (Hopscotch Films), *My Brother the Ark Raider* (BBC ALBA), Scottish BAFTA-winning *Marty Goes To Hollywood*, and BAFTA-nominated drama short *A Love Divided* (Solar Bear). The soundtrack to *A Life in Progress* was released through De-Fence Records in 2015. Band projects have included *Looper, Hoboken* and *Metrovavan*. A Looper retrospective box set was released through Mute Records in 2015.

Victoria Copeland – Assistant Director

Training: First Class BA (hons) in Performance, Northumbria University (2014).

Director and Stage Manager based in the North East.

Theatre credits include: SM for *Wor Stories* (Bravo 22 with the Royal British Legion and Newcastle Theatre Royal); SM for *We, the Crowd* (Unfolding Theatre and Sage Gateshead); ASM *The Season Ticket* (NS/Pilot Theatre co-production); Director of *Sacrè Blue*, winner of NS 'Title Pending' Award for New Theatre; ASM for *Julie* by Zinnie Harris and directed by Rebecca Frecknall; SM for *Me and Mr C* directed by Alex Swift (Gary Kitching & Co/Ovalhouse co-production); actor/onstage DSM for *Key Change* directed by Laura Lindow (Open Clasp, winner of Best Of Edinburgh Award from the Carol Tambor Theatrical Foundation and NY Times 'Critic's Pick', UK Tour, Edinburgh

Festival, National Theatre and 4th Street Theatre Workshop, New York); SM for *The Soaking of Vera Shrimp* (Live Theatre, Newcastle); ASM for *Jumping Puddles* (Open Clasp/Frantic Assembly co-production).

Faye Alvi – BSL interpreter

Faye began her early career in theatre, having trained in musical theatre and as a classically trained singer.

Having grown up with profoundly deaf parents, sign language has been a major part of her life. Re-training as a BSL/English interpreter in 2007, she wanted to be able to use her performance skills combined with BSL to offer access to deaf theatre-goers. Faye has worked on many signed performances in the north east, particularly West End touring Musicals.

The role of the integrated intepreter on stage presents a different perspective for the deaf BSL audience and allows them to freely follow the piece without missing key information.

Recent BSL integrated performances with Northern Stage include *Up and Out Christmas Sprout* and *Julie*.

For my dad, Antun Dimitrijevic.

CHARACTERS

Hedda Gabler

Jorgen Tesman

Aunty Julie

Eilert Loveborg

Thea Elvsted

Judge Brack

Berte

ACT I

A long table overflowing with flowers. **BERTE** *is dealing with them.* **AUNT JULIE** *is there.*

AUNT JULIE Do you think they are up?

BERTE No. There was a lot to unpack when they got back last night.

AUNT JULIE Good. Good. Let them have a rest.

*   **AUNT JULIE** *opens the window.*

A bit of air.

*   **BERTE** *will close it in a minute.* **AUNT JULIE** *will open it again. Possibly several times.*

*   **BERTE** *is putting flowers on the ground. She pauses.*

What is it, Berte?

BERTE What if the new mistress doesn't like me? What if she doesn't like how I do things?

AUNT JULIE She won't.

BERTE Really?

AUNT JULIE At first. But then you'll get to know each other. That's how these things go.

BERTE I hear she has some very particular habits.

AUNT JULIE And what else did you expect from General Gabler's daughter?

*   **BERTE** *is still taking flowers off the table and trying to find the right place for them.*

You know, when she was young she would gallop down the road, riding with her father.

BERTE Did she?

AUNT JULIE In a long black dress and a feather in her hat.

BERTE Mr Tesman and Hedda Gabler. Mr Tesman and...

AUNT JULIE It's "doctor" now. Dr Tesman.

They've made him a doctor while they were abroad.

BERTE I didn't know he was interested in medicine?

AUNT JULIE His doctorate is to do with books.

BERTE There.

> **BERTE** *has taken all the flowers off the table except one bunch.*

AUNT JULIE Now, why have you done that?

BERTE I was told to. They will be using this room from now on.

AUNT JULIE What? Every day?

BERTE I believe so.

AUNT JULIE Nonsense.

> **JORGEN TESMAN** *comes in. He is carrying a cup of tea with him.*

TESMAN Good morning.

AUNT JULIE Oh, good morning, my dear.

TESMAN Good morning, Aunty. You didn't have to come this early.

AUNT JULIE Of course I did. I have to make sure you are settling in.

TESMAN You probably didn't sleep at all, did you?

AUNT JULIE I don't mind.

TESMAN Did you get home all right last night?

AUNT JULIE Of course I did. Judge Brack was kind enough to see me home.

TESMAN Good. Good. I'm sorry we couldn't take you with us, but you saw how many bags Hedda had.

AUNT JULIE Yes, quite a few.

BERTE *has finished with tidying and leaves to fetch a pot of tea.*

So. How was the honeymoon?

TESMAN You'll never believe all the things I found. I went to dozens of archives, full of documents no one even knew existed.

AUNT JULIE Good. Good.

TESMAN Please, please, make yourself at home.

He helps her take the coat off.

Is that new?

AUNT JULIE I bought it for Hedda's sake.

TESMAN It's beautiful.

AUNT JULIE So she's not ashamed of me when we walk down the street.

TESMAN You do think of everything, don't you?

AUNT JULIE I try.

TESMAN Have a seat.

AUNT JULIE *is not at all sure about using this table for sitting at. She sits down anyway.*

She'll be down in a minute.

AUNT JULIE It's so good to have you back.

TESMAN I missed you, Aunty. Both you and Aunty Rina.

AUNT JULIE You know, poor Rina is not getting any better. Still not getting out of bed, poor soul. I pray I can keep her for a bit longer, especially now, now that I don't have you to look after any more.

TESMAN Come on now.

AUNT JULIE But look at you. A married man. And married to who? Hedda Gabler. The lovely Hedda Gabler. Who would have thought, with all those suitors at her door.

TESMAN Yes, who would have thought.

AUNT JULIE And what a honeymoon you've had. Five, nearly six months.

TESMAN Well, it was more of a work trip that we could take together. I had so many archives to visit. Some of those books, you can't find them anywhere else.

AUNT JULIE I can imagine.

TESMAN It was just extraordinary.

AUNT JULIE I still don't understand how you managed to pay for two.

I hear ladies can spend a fortune on a trip like this.

TESMAN Anything less wouldn't be good enough for Hedda.

AUNT JULIE I suppose. But it must have cost a lot, being away for such a long time.

TESMAN The grant covered most of it.

BERTE *brings in the tea.*

Thank you, Berte.

AUNT JULIE And no other news? Nothing else you might want to tell me?

TESMAN No, nothing really.

AUNT JULIE You would tell me, wouldn't you, if you were expecting anything else?

TESMAN Well, of course, I'm expecting a great deal. The Professorship for a start.

AUNT JULIE Of course.

TESMAN I wasn't going to say anything, but the position is as good as mine.

AUNT JULIE Good. Good.

TESMAN *pours some tea for* AUNT JULIE.

Tell me, did you manage to see much of the house?

TESMAN I have. I've been up since dawn, had a good look around.

AUNT JULIE And what do you think?

TESMAN It's wonderful. Just wonderful. All that space.

AUNT JULIE That's what I thought.

TESMAN I think we have at least two bedrooms too many. I don't know what we are going to do with them.

AUNT JULIE I'm sure you'll find some use.

TESMAN I was thinking I could make them into a library. Books, wall to wall.

AUNT JULIE Library, yes, that's what I was going to say.

TESMAN But I'm really happy for Hedda. You know she always wanted this house? She said she wouldn't be happy anywhere else.

AUNT JULIE It won't be cheap.

TESMAN Yes... I suppose it won't.

How much, what do you think? Approximately.

AUNT JULIE I couldn't tell you before all the bills come in.

TESMAN We shouldn't worry. Judge Brack arranged very good terms for the loan. He wrote to Hedda about it.

AUNT JULIE And I've put down some security...

TESMAN You did?

AUNT JULIE Well...

TESMAN What kind of security could you put down?

AUNT JULIE –

Our pensions.

TESMAN What? Your and Rina's pensions?

AUNT JULIE There was no other way.

TESMAN But that's the only income you've got.

AUNT JULIE It's just a formality, my dear. That's what Judge
Brack said. He arranged it all. Just a formality.

TESMAN Still...

AUNT JULIE Soon you'll have a good salary, and you'll be paying
the mortgage yourself. And even if we had to contribute a
bit to start with, we would be more than happy.

TESMAN Always so generous.

AUNT JULIE Nothing gives me more pleasure, my dear. It hasn't
always been easy for us, has it?

TESMAN No.

AUNT JULIE But look at us now. You are so, so close to fulfilling
your dreams.

TESMAN Isn't it remarkable how things worked out in the end?

AUNT JULIE And those that were in your way, where are they
now? Banished, that's where they are.

Especially – that one.

TESMAN Aunty.

AUNT JULIE Well Eilert Lovborg can't blame anyone else for
what has happened, can he?

TESMAN Any news on him?

AUNT JULIE Apparently he's published a book.

TESMAN Eilert Lovborg. A book?

AUNT JULIE That's what I heard.

TESMAN When?

AUNT JULIE It can't be much of a book though.

TESMAN I don't know...

AUNT JULIE Now, when your new book comes out, that will be something else.

Tell me, what is it about?

TESMAN It's about Dutch cottage industries in the Middle Ages.

AUNT JULIE Imagine that. The things you know about.

HEDDA *comes in. She just woke up.*

TESMAN And there she is.

AUNT JULIE Good morning. Good morning, my dear Hedda.

HEDDA Good morning, Miss Tesman.

Nice of you to come and visit so early.

AUNT JULIE How was the first night in your new house? Did you sleep well?

HEDDA Yes. Tolerably well.

HEDDA *pours herself some tea.*

TESMAN Ha! You were sleeping like a log.

HEDDA It's far too bright for this time of day.

AUNT JULIE Let's close the window then.

TESMAN *gets up to do it.*

HEDDA Don't. Draw the curtains instead, it gives a nicer light.

TESMAN Here we go, now we have both shade and fresh air.

HEDDA *(looking at all the flowers)* And with all of these we will need some air.

AUNT JULIE *gets up.*

Miss Tesman, please, sit down.

AUNT JULIE Thank you my dear, but now that I can see things are going well here, I better head home. Back to my poor sister.

TESMAN Give her all my love, will you? Tell her I'll come for a visit, later today.

HEDDA *is looking at all the flowers, not sure why they are all there. Not sure why she is there either.*

AUNT JULIE Oh, I almost forgot. I have something for you. Here.

TESMAN What's that?

She hands him a parcel. He opens it.

Good Lord, you kept them for me. Hedda!

HEDDA Yes?

TESMAN How kind of you, Aunt Julie.

HEDDA What are those?

TESMAN My old slippers.

TESMAN *hugs* **AUNT JULIE**. *The time stops just for a moment and* **HEDDA** *can clearly see* **TESMAN** *delighted over a pair of old slippers. It all goes back to normal.*

HEDDA Yes. He mentioned them a lot while we were away.

TESMAN I missed them so much. Here, have a look.

HEDDA It's all right. I'm fine.

TESMAN Aunt Rina embroidered them for me. She must have been working all through her illness. You can't imagine how many memories are wrapped up in these.

HEDDA No, I don't think I can.

AUNT JULIE It's different for Hedda, my dear.

TESMAN I know, I know. But she's part of the family now.

HEDDA I don't think we'll get on with this maid.

AUNT JULIE With Berte?

TESMAN Why wouldn't we?

HEDDA Look. She left her old coat just laying around.

TESMAN Hedda –

HEDDA Imagine if someone came in and saw it.

TESMAN Hedda, that is Aunty Julie's coat.

HEDDA Is it?

AUNT JULIE Yes, it is. And it's certainly not old, my dear.

HEDDA I really didn't look at it very closely.

AUNT JULIE Brand new, in fact. This is the first time I had it on.

TESMAN It really is a very nice coat. Beautiful.

AUNT JULIE Thank you, my dear. But it's not necessary.

HEDDA It's lovely.

AUNT JULIE *picks up her coat.*

AUNT JULIE I'd better go now.

TESMAN Before you go, won't you have a look at Hedda? How lovely she is.

AUNT JULIE That's nothing new my dear. Hedda has been lovely all her life.

TESMAN Have you noticed how she's filled up while we were away?

HEDDA Really?

AUNT JULIE Has she?

TESMAN You might not be able to see it just now, but I have had opportunity...

HEDDA Would you / please stop it ...

TESMAN It will be the mountain air.

HEDDA I haven't changed a bit since the day we left.

TESMAN That's what you say. But you can't see yourself. What do you say, Aunty?

HEDDA Stop it.

AUNT JULIE Lovely. She is very lovely.

AUNT JULIE gives HEDDA a hug.

God bless you, Hedda Gabler. God bless you both.

HEDDA Thank you, Miss Tesman.

AUNT JULIE I'll come and visit every single day.

HEDDA Wonderful.

AUNT JULIE Well goodbye now, my dears. Goodbye.

As they are leaving.

TESMAN Here. I'll see you out...

They leave. HEDDA looks at the flowers, at the room, at the table, out of the window. How did she end up here?

TESMAN *comes back.*

What are you looking at?

HEDDA Nothing.

TESMAN Did Aunty Julie seem all right to you? She was strangely formal.

HEDDA I barely know her. Is she usually any different?

TESMAN She wasn't her usual self.

HEDDA Do you think she was offended by what I said about the coat?

TESMAN Not for too long.

HEDDA It's not good manners to just throw your things like that. People don't do such things.

TESMAN She won't do it again.

HEDDA Anyway, I'll smooth it out with her.

TESMAN That would be very kind of you.

HEDDA When you go and see them later, why don't you invite her out here for the evening?

TESMAN I know what would make her even happier.

HEDDA What would that be?

TESMAN Could you call her "Aunty"?

HEDDA You can't ask me that, Tesman. I've told you, I'll call her, "Aunt Julie" but that is it.

TESMAN I just thought, as you are now part of the family...

HEDDA *is looking at the window.* Hmm...

Is something wrong?

HEDDA These curtains. They don't really fit in here.

TESMAN As soon as I start getting my salary we can get rid of them.

HEDDA No. We can put them in the other room, and we'll put the new ones here instead.

When we can, of course.

TESMAN Yes, we can certainly do that.

HEDDA *(noticing a bunch of flowers)* These weren't here last night?

TESMAN I think Aunty Julie brought them for you.

HEDDA *takes out the card.*

HEDDA "I'll come and visit later in the day."

Can you guess who they're from?

TESMAN Who?

HEDDA Mrs Elvsted.

TESMAN Really? Ms Rysing?

HEDDA She is Mrs Elvsted now.

TESMAN Of course.

HEDDA Her with her irritating hair.

TESMAN –

HEDDA I heard you two used to be...an item?

TESMAN Oh, that was years ago. Before I knew you. And it didn't really last that long.

HEDDA I see.

TESMAN Imagine her being in town.

HEDDA Why might she be coming to see us? I barely remember her from school.

TESMAN I haven't seen her for...for years. I don't know how she can stand it, up there, in the country.

HEDDA Hasn't she been living in the same town as Eilert Lovborg?

TESMAN Actually she has.

BERTE *enters.*

BERTE She is here again, madam. The lady that left those earlier.

BERTE *is referring to the flowers in* **HEDDA***'s hand.*

HEDDA Is she? Well, let her in.

BERTE *leaves.* **HEDDA** *and* **TESMAN** *are on their own.*

TESMAN What?

HEDDA Nothing.

BERTE *lets* **MRS ELVSTED** *in.*

Good morning, my dear Mrs Elvsted. Lovely to see you again.

MRS ELVSTED You too Mrs Tesman. It's been so long.

TESMAN So long.

HEDDA Thank you so much for these lovely flowers.

MRS ELVSTED Oh, don't mention it. I would have come at once, but then I heard you were still away.

I was desperate to see you.

TESMAN My dear Ms Rysing –

HEDDA Mrs Elvsted.

TESMAN Of course, / Mrs Elvsted...

HEDDA Is there something wrong?

MRS ELVSTED In fact, there is and no one else who can help me, but you.

HEDDA Come. Let's sit down.

MRS ELVSTED I'm too upset to be sitting down.

HEDDA Nonsense. Please. Sit down.

MRS ELVSTED *sits down.*

TESMAN So...what is it, / Ms Rys –

HEDDA Has something happened at home?

MRS ELVSTED Well, it has. And it hasn't.

HEDDA All right.

MRS ELVSTED I really, really don't want you to misunderstand me –

HEDDA The best thing to do then, is to tell us what is going on.

MRS ELVSTED –

In case you didn't know, Eilert Lovborg is also in town.

HEDDA Lovborg?

TESMAN So Lovborg is back in town? Did you hear that, Hedda?

HEDDA I did.

MRS ELVSTED He's been here for a week. A whole week in this town full of temptations.

HEDDA But dear Mrs Elvsted, what does that have to do with you?

MRS ELVSTED He's been tutoring my children.

HEDDA Your children?

MRS ELVSTED My husband's children. I don't have any myself.

HEDDA I see.

TESMAN So was he – I don't know how else to say this, so I'm just going to say it – was he sober enough to be employed as a tutor?

MRS ELVSTED He's been a model citizen for the last few years.

TESMAN Really? Did you hear this, Hedda?

HEDDA Yes. I did.

MRS ELVSTED There's not a thing you could say against him. But still, knowing he is here and with so much money on him – now, that really scares me.

HEDDA Does it?

BERTE *brings more tea.*

MRS ELVSTED Once his book came out, he just couldn't stay still.

TESMAN Oh yes, Aunty Julie said he published a book.

MRS ELVSTED A significant book on social and political history. It was published just a few weeks ago, and so many people have already read it. I believe, it's caused quite a stir.

TESMAN It must have been an old manuscript he had laying around.

MRS ELVSTED Oh, no. He wrote the whole thing while he was staying with us. It took him about a year, not more.

TESMAN That's good / to hear.

HEDDA So have you seen him, since you've been in town?

MRS ELVSTED Not yet. I didn't know where he was staying, but now finally I have the address.

HEDDA And how come your husband / didn't come with...

MRS ELVSTED / What about my husband?

HEDDA How come he sent you on your own? I thought he might come down himself, look for his friend.

MRS ELVSTED Oh, he doesn't have time for that. And I had to buy a few things anyway...

HEDDA Well then. That makes complete sense.

MRS ELVSTED I beg you, Mr Tesman. When he visits, will you receive him kindly?

TESMAN Well, I don't know / if he would...

MRS ELVSTED He will. You used to be such good friends.

TESMAN We were. Yes.

MRS ELVSTED Please, would you?

The time stops for a few moments and HEDDA *can see clearly that her husband and* MRS ELVSTED *have a history she doesn't know anything about. It lasts just for a few brief moments, and then everything goes back to normal.*

TESMAN It will be my pleasure, Ms Rysing.

HEDDA Elvsted.

TESMAN I'll do whatever I can for Eilert. You can count on that.

MRS ELVSTED Thank you. Thank you.

HEDDA Why don't you write and invite him, Tesman? He might not come to see you otherwise.

TESMAN That's a good idea.

HEDDA Sooner rather than later, I'd say.

MRS ELVSTED If only you would.

TESMAN I'll do it right now. Do you have his address, Ms – Mrs Elvsted?

MRS ELVSTED Here.

TESMAN Right then. Where are my...ah, there they are.

TESMAN *takes his slippers/parcel.*

HEDDA Make sure it's a kind and friendly letter, will you? It can't just be a short one.

TESMAN Of course not.

MRS ELVSTED But please, don't tell him I was asking on his behalf.

TESMAN I wouldn't dream of it.

TESMAN *leaves.*

HEDDA There. Two birds with one stone.

MRS ELVSTED What do you mean?

HEDDA I wanted him out of the way.

MRS ELVSTED So he can go and write the letter?

HEDDA So you and I can talk.

MRS ELVSTED About the letter?

HEDDA Yes. Fine. About the letter.

MRS ELVSTED I don't know if there is much else to be said, Mrs Tesman.

HEDDA Of course there is. So much more. Come, let's sit down.

MRS ELVSTED I should really be going...

HEDDA Nonsense. Tell me more. How are things at home?

MRS ELVSTED That's the last thing I'd like tell anyone about.

HEDDA But surely, you can tell me. We went to school together.

MRS ELVSTED Yes, but you were a year above me. I was terribly frightened of you then.

HEDDA Of me?

MRS ELVSTED If we met at the stairs you'd always pull my hair.

HEDDA No? Did I?

MRS ELVSTED And once you said you'll burn it all off.

HEDDA Oh that was just a joke.

MRS ELVSTED And then after school...we went separate ways. Our lives ended up being so very different.

HEDDA Well then, we should make sure we get close again. Listen, we used to call each other by our first names.

MRS ELVSTED I'm quite sure we didn't.

HEDDA Nonsense. I remember it quite clearly. And now we are friends again, we will call each other by our first names. You will call me Hedda and I will call you Thora.

MRS ELVSTED Thea.

HEDDA Of course. Thea.

MRS ELVSTED Yes.

HEDDA So. Thea. How are things at home?

MRS ELVSTED What home? I don't think I ever really had one.

HEDDA I knew there was something wrong.

MRS ELVSTED There is, yes.

HEDDA Didn't you move up to be Mr Elvsted's housekeeper? At the beginning.

And then, in the end, you became the mistress of the house?

MRS ELVSTED Yes. I did.

HEDDA And it's been...how long now?

MRS ELVSTED Five years since I got married.

HEDDA Five years.

MRS ELVSTED And the last few...if you could only imagine, Mrs Tesman.

HEDDA Now, Thea.

MRS ELVSTED I'm sorry. Hedda. If you could only imagine.

HEDDA And Eilert has been up for the last few years, isn't that right?

MRS ELVSTED Eilert Lovborg? Yes, I believe so.

HEDDA So did you know him already?

MRS ELVSTED Well, I've heard of him, of course.

HEDDA But then, up there, he'd come to your house?

MRS ELVSTED Every day. You see, he was going to teach the children. In the end I couldn't do it all on my own.

HEDDA Of course not. And your husband...? I suppose he was often working away?

MRS ELVSTED He was. His work takes him all over the district.

HEDDA Oh Thea. My poor Thea. You must tell me everything. All of it.

MRS ELVSTED What would you like to know, Mrs... I mean, Hedda.

HEDDA What kind of man is your husband really? What is he like to be with?

Is he good to you?

MRS ELVSTED I think he believes he is doing the right thing.

HEDDA But?

MRS ELVSTED But there is very little I like about him. He is twenty years older than me and we don't have one thing in common – not a thing.

HEDDA I'm sure he still cares about you, in his own way?

MRS ELVSTED I think he finds me useful. And it doesn't cost much to keep me. I'm cheap.

HEDDA What a silly thing to say.

MRS ELVSTED That's how he sees the world. I don't think he cares about anyone else but himself. Maybe about his children a bit.

HEDDA And of course, about Eilert Lovborg.

MRS ELVSTED What on earth makes you think that?

HEDDA I just assumed, as he sent you all this way to find him...

MRS ELVSTED Yes.

HEDDA Isn't that what you just told Tesman?

MRS ELVSTED –

Oh, I might as well tell you. It will come out sooner or later.

HEDDA Yes?

MRS ELVSTED My husband doesn't know I left.

HEDDA What do you mean he doesn't know?

MRS ELVSTED He's away again. And I just couldn't stand it anymore. I knew I'd lose my mind being up there all on my own.

HEDDA So...

MRS ELVSTED So I packed a few things. And left.

HEDDA You left?

MRS ELVSTED Yes.

HEDDA Just like that?

MRS ELVSTED Took the train right into town.

HEDDA Were you not scared?

MRS ELVSTED What else could I do?

HEDDA And what do you think he will say when you get back home?

MRS ELVSTED Oh, I'm never going back there.

HEDDA You mean, you left him for good?

MRS ELVSTED Yes.

HEDDA And so openly.

MRS ELVSTED It's not like I could hide that kind of thing.

HEDDA But what will people say?

MRS ELVSTED I don't care. Let them say whatever they want to say.

HEDDA –

MRS ELVSTED I did what I had to do. That's all.

HEDDA And what now? What happens next?

MRS ELVSTED I don't know yet. The only thing I know is I need to be where Eilert Lovborg is. If I am to be at all.

HEDDA Tell me, Thea, how did this...this friendship, between you Eilert. How did that happen?

MRS ELVSTED Slowly. Little by little. It was as if I was gaining some sort of power over him.

HEDDA Really?

MRS ELVSTED He gave up all his old habits. And not because I asked him to, I'd never dare do that. But he must have noticed what I didn't like, so he would give it up.

HEDDA You made a new man out of him?

MRS ELVSTED That's what he says.

And he, for his part, he's made a new person out of me. He taught me to think, to understand the world.

HEDDA So he was teaching you as well as the children?

MRS ELVSTED Not really. He talked to me. Like an equal. About so many different things. And then with time, I started working with him. Whenever he was writing, we would work together.

HEDDA You mean, as good friends?

MRS ELVSTED Friends, colleagues...that's what he'd say.

HEDDA Friends.

MRS ELVSTED I know I should be happy, but I just can't. I don't think all this will end well.

HEDDA I thought you would have more confidence in him?

MRS ELVSTED –

HEDDA What?

MRS ELVSTED You see, there is a shadow of a woman standing between Eilert and me.

HEDDA Really? Who?

MRS ELVSTED I don't know. Someone from his past.

Someone he can't seem to forget.

HEDDA Has he said anything else?

MRS ELVSTED Only once, he mentioned her very briefly.

HEDDA What did he say?

MRS ELVSTED Apparently, when they parted she threatened to shoot him with a pistol.

HEDDA Nonsense. People don't do such things. Not around here.

MRS ELVSTED That's why I think it's that red-haired singer / he once was –

HEDDA Yes! It will be her.

MRS ELVSTED I hear she goes around with a loaded pistol.

HEDDA Well there you go. It must be her.

TESMAN *comes in carrying a letter.*

TESMAN There we are. All finished and ready to go.

MRS ELVSTED Please don't mention (any of this)...

HEDDA Mrs Elvsted was just leaving.

BERTE *enters.*

BERTE Judge Brack is here. He is asking if he can welcome back Mr and Mrs Tesman?

HEDDA Let him in please.

BERTE *lets him in.*

JUDGE BRACK May one dare to call so early in the day?

HEDDA Yes, indeed, one may.

At the same time.

TESMAN Berte, could you maybe take care of this for me?

BERTE Of course, Mr Tesman.

BERTE *takes the letter. She leaves.*

TESMAN You know you are always welcome to our house.

Judge Brack, Ms Rysing.

HEDDA Oh for (*fuck's sake*)...

BRACK My pleasure.

HEDDA It's strange to see you in the daylight, Judge.

BRACK Do you find me...different?

HEDDA A touch younger, I'd say.

BRACK Well, thank you.

MRS ELVSTED I should / really be going...

TESMAN And what do you say about Hedda? Isn't she just glowing?

HEDDA Would you stop it already?

TESMAN I was / just saying that you are glowing.

MRS ELVSTED I / will just...

HEDDA You could thank Judge Brack for all the trouble he's gone through.

BRACK No need to mention it.

HEDDA You've been a great friend to us.

BRACK It was a pleasure.

HEDDA I believe Mrs Elvsted wishes to leave. I won't be a minute.

Goodbyes. HEDDA *and* MRS ELVSTED *leave.*

BRACK So? I assume your lovely wife is happy with the arrangements?

TESMAN We can't thank you enough.

BRACK But?

TESMAN But it looks like we might have to rearrange a thing or two. And there might be few things missing. I suppose we'll still have to make a couple of purchases.

BRACK Really?

TESMAN But don't worry, none of that will be your problem. Hedda will take care of it all herself.

Please sit down. Thank you, thank you. Etc.

BRACK Have a seat.

TESMAN Is it time for a serious conversation?

BRACK No, no need to worry about finances yet. Though I wish you arranged things a bit more modestly.

TESMAN That wasn't an option. I wouldn't do that to Hedda.

BRACK And therein lies our problem.

TESMAN Luckily, it won't be long before I get my appointment.

BRACK You know, those things sometimes take longer than expected.

TESMAN Why? Have you heard something?

BRACK Nothing definite.

TESMAN But...

BRACK But there is a bit of news I need to share with you.

TESMAN What is it?

BRACK Your old friend Eilert Lovborg is back in town.

TESMAN I know.

BRACK Really? Who told you?

TESMAN Hedda's friend, the one you just met.

BRACK Yes, of course, the magistrate's wife. Hasn't he been staying with them, up north?

TESMAN He has. And, from what I hear, he's become a respectable man once again.

BRACK Yes, that's the rumour.

TESMAN He's also published a new book.

BRACK I heard.

TESMAN It's attracting a lot of attention.

HEDDA *comes in.*

BRACK Yes, a surprising amount of attention.

TESMAN Isn't that wonderful? He was always so talented. I was certain there was no coming back for him.

BRACK That's what we all thought.

TESMAN Although I can't imagine how he is making a living.

Time stops again. This time for longer. HEDDA *knows she has a few moments to observe the situation. She looks at the two men having a serious conversation. She joins them at the table. She mimics their posture. She goes back to her place. Time starts again.*

HEDDA Tesman is always worried about making a living.

TESMAN I was talking about the poor Lovborg.

HEDDA Were you? What about him?

TESMAN Well, I heard that his inheritance was long gone. And he can't possibly write a new book every year. So I was just wondering...what is going to happen to him.

BRACK His family are still pretty influential.

TESMAN No, they've washed their hands off a long time ago.

HEDDA Have they? After all, the Elvsteds seem to have made a new man out of him.

BRACK And he's got a new book coming out...

TESMAN I really do hope that book helps him. I just wrote to him, asked him to come and visit us this evening.

BRACK I thought you were coming to my party tonight?

HEDDA Have you forgotten?

TESMAN Actually, I have.

BRACK It doesn't matter, he wouldn't come here anyway.

HEDDA Why do you think so?

BRACK Well... I suppose you'll find out one way or another.

TESMAN What is it?

BRACK Your appointment might not come as soon as you were expecting.

TESMAN Why not?

BRACK The position might have to be open to the competition.

HEDDA How interesting.

TESMAN But who could I be competing with – you don't mean...

BRACK With Eilert Lovborg.

TESMAN Impossible.

BRACK Improbable, yes. Impossible, no.

TESMAN That's so inconsiderate.

Hedda and I, we got married on those expectations. We arranged a loan. We got into debt. We even borrowed from my aunt!

They practically promised me that appointment.

BRACK I have no doubt, in the end, it will be you who gets the appointment.

But there will have to be a contest.

HEDDA A duel.

TESMAN How can you joke about it?

HEDDA I'm not joking. I can't wait to see who is going to win.

BRACK Either way, at least now you know. I mean...before you make any other purchases.

BRACK *gets up to go.*

HEDDA This won't change anything.

BRACK I just thought I should tell you. So, there.

TESMAN So there.

BRACK I better go.

(*To* TESMAN) I'll come and collect you after my walk this afternoon.

TESMAN Yes. I suppose.

HEDDA Goodbye, Judge Brack. Do come and visit us again.

BRACK With pleasure. Goodbye. Goodbye.

BRACK *leaves.*

TESMAN Oh Hedda, why did we get carried away?

HEDDA Did we?

TESMAN It was stupid to get married and into debt, all on a promise.

HEDDA Yes. You might be right.

TESMAN At least we have our beautiful home. The quiet home we both wanted so much.

HEDDA A home in which we can entertain. That was the agreement.

TESMAN I was so looking forward to that. You would have made a wonderful hostess.

HEDDA "Would have"?

TESMAN Well for now, that just won't be possible. It will have to be just you and I. And Aunty Julie from time to time.

HEDDA So that means no parties?

TESMAN I'm afraid not. We just can't afford that now.

HEDDA And I can't travel to visit friends?

TESMAN Travel?

HEDDA I suppose that is out of the question too?

TESMAN That goes without saying.

HEDDA Well, at least I have one thing to cheer me up.

TESMAN Thank God for that. And what's that?

HEDDA My pistols, Jorgen.

TESMAN Pistols?

HEDDA General Gabler's pistols.

TESMAN Don't touch those things. They are dangerous.

HEDDA Are they?

She leaves, he goes after her.

TESMAN So dangerous. Hedda, please don't.

ACT II

Afternoon. **HEDDA** *is loading a pistol. Another one is next to it. She shoots out of the window. She shoots at the flowers in the room. She is about to shoot at one of the chairs.*

JUDGE BRACK *appears.*

HEDDA Good afternoon, Judge!

BRACK Good afternoon, Mrs Tesman!

HEDDA And now I shoot you, Judge Brack!

She shoots.

BRACK Would you stop shooting!

HEDDA That's what you get for sneaking in the back way.

She shoots.

HEDDA Are you coming in then?

BRACK Will you stop shooting!

HEDDA I might.

JUDGE BRACK *comes in. He is dressed for the party.*

BRACK I can't believe you are still playing with these.

HEDDA Not a game Judge Brack.

BRACK What were you shooting at?

HEDDA The blue sky.

HEDDA *doesn't put the gun down.*

Do you know Judge Brack, what wild ducks do, if wounded by a gun?

BRACK I can't say I do.

HEDDA They dive to the bottom of the lake, as deep as they can get, and bite themselves fast in the tangle and seaweed. They never come up again.

BRACK (*takes the guns from her*) No more of that.

HEDDA Tell me, what else am I supposed to do with myself?

BRACK Have you had no visitors?

HEDDA Not one.

BRACK And Tesman is not home either?

HEDDA *locks the pistols back into the box.*

HEDDA As soon as he's eaten, he's run off to the aunts. He wasn't expecting you so early.

BRACK Well if I knew he wouldn't be here, I would have come earlier.

HEDDA Then you wouldn't have found anyone here. I was in my room, getting dressed.

BRACK There must be a little crack in the door, no? We could have talked through it.

HEDDA No, I believe you forgot to arrange one.

BRACK How foolish of me.

HEDDA Well, we'll just have to talk here. While we wait for Tesman.

BRACK I'm in no rush.

HEDDA *and* **BRACK** *both sit and wait.*

HEDDA Well?

BRACK Well?

HEDDA I asked first.

BRACK Shall we talk?

HEDDA Don't you think it's been ages since we had a proper conversation?

BRACK I've been walking by, every day, hoping you'll be back soon.

HEDDA So did I. The whole time.

BRACK Really? I thought you were having wonderful time on your honeymoon.

HEDDA I'm not surprised.

BRACK Tesman said so in his letters.

HEDDA He was having a wonderful time. He thinks there's nothing more exciting than spending twelve hours in a dusty archive.

BRACK Well, it is his passion and his profession, after all.

HEDDA But it's not my passion, is it? The whole thing was so excruciatingly dull.

BRACK Do you really mean that?

HEDDA Imagine spending six months, without once talking to anyone you know, or even anyone who knows anyone you know. Someone you can really talk to, like you and I do.

BRACK Yes, I can see how that would be difficult.

HEDDA And that wasn't the worst thing either.

BRACK No? What was it?

HEDDA Having to spend every single minute of the day – with the same person.

BRACK Every day. And every night.

HEDDA Every moment of every single day.

BRACK But Tesman is so generous and kind...

HEDDA He's an academic.

BRACK That, he is.

HEDDA And academics are not fun to travel with. Not for this stretch of time anyway.

BRACK Not even if it's an academic you love?

HEDDA Oh, don't use that stupid word.

BRACK Mrs Hedda.

HEDDA What? You should try it yourself.

Listening to nothing else but a medieval history, every morning and every evening...

BRACK Every moment of every single day.

HEDDA Exactly! I know so much about cruck houses and thatched roofs and all there is to know about wattle and daub. Do I really want to know about any of that?

BRACK So, how did all this happen then?

HEDDA How did I end up with Jorgen Tesman?

BRACK Yes, let's put it that way.

HEDDA I danced myself out, my dear Judge. I ran out of time.

BRACK Don't say such things.

HEDDA And you can't deny that Tesman is a very respectable man.

BRACK Both respectable and dependable.

HEDDA He is a very diligent researcher. With time, who knows, he might get far.

BRACK He might.

HEDDA And he was so desperate to be the one allowed to provide for me. Tell me, why should I reject that?

BRACK Well, when you put it that way...

HEDDA That was much more than any other suitor was willing to do, my dear Judge.

BRACK I can't speak for the others, but as far as I am concerned, you know I have always respected the institution of marriage from afar. In theory, as it were, Mrs Hedda.

HEDDA Oh, I've never entertained any hopes of you, my dear Judge.

BRACK All I desire is to have a good circle of intimate friends, where I can be of service in word and deed, and allowed to come and go as a trusted friend.

HEDDA As a friend of a man of the house?

BRACK Preferably, of the woman. But next to that, of the man as well, if possible.

HEDDA If possible.

BRACK That kind of "triangular relationship" can be deeply satisfying for all the parties.

HEDDA There were certainly times when I was feeling the lack of the third on our long journey. With just the two of us, alone in the compartment...

BRACK Luckily the honeymoon is now over and done...

HEDDA This journey is far from over, my judge. I've just reached one of the stations.

BRACK Well then one might think about jumping off the train for a bit. Stretching one's legs a little.

HEDDA I'll never jump off, Judge Brack.

BRACK Are you sure?

HEDDA Yes. Because there's always someone...

BRACK Who might see you jumping off?

HEDDA Exactly.

BRACK And what if the third person was to step in to the compartment to join the couple?

HEDDA Well, that would be something else.

BRACK A tried, trusted, understanding friend...

HEDDA ...able to converse on all sorts of subjects...

BRACK ...and not even a little bit academic.

HEDDA That would be a relief.

TESMAN *shows up at the door.*

TESMAN Judge Brack, good afternoon.

HEDDA And the train goes on.

TESMAN *is carrying a number of paperbacks.*

TESMAN These just get heavier in the heat. I'm sweating like a pig, Hedda. Look.

JUDGE Good afternoon.

HEDDA *(re books)* What on earth are these?

TESMAN New academic quarterlies. I just had to have them.

HEDDA Academic quarterlies.

BRACK Yes, academic, Mrs Hedda.

HEDDA Do you really need any more journals?

TESMAN Well they are new. I must keep up with what's being written and published.

HEDDA I suppose you do.

TESMAN And here, I managed to get Eilert's new book as well.

Do you want to have a look?

HEDDA Maybe later.

TESMAN I read a few pages on my way back.

BRACK And what do you think, as an academic?

TESMAN Remarkably thoughtful. He never used to write like this. It will be a joy to read. And I should probably change. We don't have to leave right away, do we?

BRACK No. No need to rush.

TESMAN Wonderful, I'll take my time then.

> **TESMAN** *is about to leave then stops.*

I almost forgot, Hedda, Aunty Julie won't be coming to see you tonight.

HEDDA Is it because of what happened with the coat?

TESMAN Of course not, how can you say that? Aunt Rina is poorly, she can't leave her on her own.

HEDDA Isn't she always poorly?

TESMAN Well today she is particularly unwell.

HEDDA In that case, what can we can do? I'll just have to manage on my own.

TESMAN But Aunty Julie is so happy to see you thriving. So happy.

HEDDA Those eternal aunts.

TESMAN Sorry?

HEDDA Nothing.

TESMAN All right then.

> **TESMAN** *leaves.*

BRACK What was that about the coat?

HEDDA Nothing really. She left her coat on the chair and I pretended I thought it was the maid's.

BRACK Did you really?

HEDDA I did.

BRACK And to do that to such a nice old lady.

HEDDA I know. It just comes over me, and I can't resist it. I don't know why.

BRACK You are unhappy, Hedda. That's what that is.

HEDDA Why should I be happy? Can you tell me? What do I have to make me happy?

BRACK Well, for a start you have the house you always wanted.

HEDDA You didn't believe that story, did you?

BRACK Isn't it true?

HEDDA Very little of it.

BRACK How come?

HEDDA Last summer, if you remember, I was using Tesman to see me home from all the parties.

BRACK Unfortunately, last summer I was going in the other direction.

HEDDA You certainly were.

BRACK Shame on you, Mrs Hedda.

HEDDA Anyway, one evening we were passing this house and Tesman, poor thing, he just run out of things to say. He couldn't find anything to talk about. So I took pity on the erudite creature...

BRACK You did?

HEDDA I most certainly did. And to help him out of his embarrassment, I just happened to say – on an impulse – that I'd quite like to live here.

BRACK And that was all?

HEDDA That's all I said that night.

BRACK And later?

HEDDA It turns out my impulsiveness had consequences.

BRACK Unfortunately, it often does.

HEDDA We somehow bonded over that conversation, a conversation about a house, which then led to more conversations, which then led to the engagement, which then led to the wedding and the honeymoon and to all this.

BRACK So you don't really care for this house?

HEDDA Not one bit.

BRACK Not even now they've made it so pretty for you.

HEDDA What am I supposed to do with"pretty"?

The whole place smells of lavender and rose petals. But then again, that might be Aunt Julie.

–

Look at it. This place is going to bore me to death.

BRACK I'm sure life will provide you with an exciting challenge. Any day now.

HEDDA I often think about what that might be. There is one thing...

BRACK Go on.

HEDDA I'd like to get Tesman into politics.

BRACK Tesman? Into politics? That's a world he doesn't care for. Or know anything about.

HEDDA I know, I know. But what if I could still persuade him?

BRACK What satisfaction would that bring to you? If he is not interested, why would you want him to do it?

HEDDA What other option do I have? Tell me, what else is there for me to do here?

BRACK My dear / Mrs Hedda...

HEDDA So you think it's completely out of the question for Tesman to become a prime minister?

BRACK He would have to be a fairly rich man.

HEDDA There you go. That's the problem. Money.

BRACK I don't think that's the problem.

HEDDA Well what is the problem then?

BRACK I don't think you were ever really challenged by life.

HEDDA I wasn't?

BRACK But, who knows, there might be something in your near future. Some unexpected demands on your time?

HEDDA That is not going to happen.

BRACK I'd say, it will happen within a year.

HEDDA I have no desire for such things, Judge Brack. Not for that kind of thing.

BRACK But you must. Surely, every woman feels the urge to...

HEDDA Enough!

Sometimes I feel I have only one urge.

BRACK And what is that, if I can ask?

HEDDA To bore myself to death as quickly as possible.

BRACK –

HEDDA So there. Now you know.

–

And here is the professor.

TESMAN *enters.*

TESMAN Hedda, Eilert hasn't sent us a message, has he?

HEDDA No.

TESMAN In that case, he'll be here any moment.

BRACK Do you really think he will come here?

TESMAN I am certain he will. And I am certain what we heard this morning was just an ugly rumour.

BRACK Really?

TESMAN Aunty Julie thinks he wouldn't stand in my way.

BRACK In that case, it must be true.

TESMAN We should really wait for him, as long as we can.

BRACK There's plenty of time. No one is coming before seven thirty.

TESMAN In that case, we'll keep Hedda company and see what happens.

HEDDA And if the worst comes to the worst, Mr Lovborg can always settle down here with me.

TESMAN I don't think it would be proper for him to be here if Aunty Julie is not coming.

HEDDA But Mrs Elvsted is. So the three of us can have tea.

TESMAN Oh, in that case, that's all right.

BRACK A "healthier" option for him as well.

HEDDA Judge...

BRACK Haven't you mocked my parties at every occasion? Don't you say they are suitable for the men of strong will only?

HEDDA Surely, Mr Lovborg is a man of strong will. As a reformed sinner –

BERTE *enters.*

BERTE Madam, there is a gentleman who would like to come in –

HEDDA Well, let him come in then.

TESMAN That must be him.

EILERT LOVBORG *enters. He bows.*

Oh no, my dear Eilert. *(He shakes his hand)* Finally, we meet again.

LOVBORG Thank you for the letter.

Offers his hand to HEDDA.

Mrs Tesman.

HEDDA *(she accepts the handshake)* Welcome, Mr Lovborg.

I don't know if you two / gentlemen have met.

LOVBORG Judge Brack, I believe.

BRACK Heavens. It was years ago...

TESMAN Please, make yourself at home. Hedda and I insist. Don't we?

HEDDA Of course.

TESMAN I hear you are planning to move back to town?

LOVBORG I am. Yes.

TESMAN Makes sense. I managed to have a look at your new book, but I just haven't had time to properly read it yet.

LOVBORG Don't bother with it.

TESMAN Why's that?

LOVBORG There's really not much to it.

TESMAN How can you say that?

BRACK I hear it's getting wonderful reviews.

LOVBORG That was my aim. I wanted to write something popular, something anyone could like fairly easily.

BRACK Very sensible.

TESMAN But, / my dear Eilert...

LOVBORG / You see, I had to rebuild my reputation. Something to allow me to start again.

TESMAN Well, that makes sense.

LOVBORG *has a manuscript with him.*

LOVBORG But when this one comes out. That will be the one to read.

This is the real one. The one that is really – me.

TESMAN Really? What is it about?

LOVBORG It's the sequel.

TESMAN Of what?

LOVBORG Of my current book.

TESMAN The new one?

LOVBORG Yes.

TESMAN But that one goes all the way to our times?

LOVBORG Yes, it does. And this one is about the future.

TESMAN But we don't know anything about the future.

LOVBORG And there's so much to be said about it anyway.

Here, it's divided / in two parts...

TESMAN That is not your handwriting.

LOVBORG I dictated it. It's divided into two parts.

The first is about various powers that will shape our society in the future. And the second is about the direction our society will take under those powers. Here.

LOVBORG hands TESMAN the book. TESMAN leans over to read some of it. The time stops. HEDDA stands up and looks at the scene. Two men hunched over a book. One reading, one waiting for the verdict. She looks at the scene from different sides. She sees things a bit more clearly. The time starts again.

TESMAN Incredible.

HEDDA Isn't it.

TESMAN I would never think to write about something like that.

HEDDA No. You wouldn't.

LOVBORG I brought it with me, I thought, maybe I could read you some of it tonight.

TESMAN That's very thoughtful of you, but tonight might not be the best...

LOVBORG Some other time then. There is no rush.

BRACK Mr Lovborg, there is a little party at my house this evening. And what Tesman is trying to say –

LOVBORG My apologies...

BRACK No, no, no. I was going to say, would you do us the pleasure of joining us?

LOVBORG I can't. No. But thank you.

BRACK It will be a small, select circle. And we shall have a "jolly" time, as Hed – Mrs Tesman likes to say.

LOVBORG I don't doubt it.

BRACK So?

LOVBORG Still no. But, thank you.

BRACK Why don't you bring the manuscript with you, you could read it to Tesman over there. I have more than enough rooms.

TESMAN That's a wonderful idea.

HEDDA I don't think Mr Lovborg really wants to, my dear.

TESMAN What do you say, Eilert?

HEDDA I think he would rather stay here, and have supper with me.

LOVBORG Supper with you, Mrs Tesman?

HEDDA And with Mrs Elvsted, of course.

LOVBORG Ah. I saw her briefly at lunchtime.

HEDDA Did you?

LOVBORG Yes, very briefly.

HEDDA Well she's coming over in a bit, so in fact, it is essential you stay, otherwise who is going to see her home?

LOVBORG That's true.

HEDDA Yes.

LOVBORG In that case, it will be my pleasure to stay. Thank you.

HEDDA I'll tell the maid.

She goes to get **BERTE**. *She talks to* **BERTE** *while the men talk.*

TESMAN So Eilert, this new subject of yours – the future. Is that something you might be lecturing on?

LOVBORG It is. Yes.

TESMAN They told me at the bookshop you will be giving a series of lectures this autumn.

LOVBORG I would like to, yes. You musn't blame me for that, Tesman.

TESMAN Oh, of course not.

LOVBORG I see how this might be awkward for you.

TESMAN I couldn't possibly ask you not to. Not for my sake.

LOVBORG Of course, I'll wait until you've been appointed.

TESMAN You'll wait?

LOVBORG I will.

TESMAN So you won't be competing with me for the post?

LOVBORG No. I intend to outdo you only in reputation.

TESMAN So Aunty Julie was right. Hedda, did you hear that? Lovborg won't stand in our way.

HEDDA "Our" way?

TESMAN What do you say to all this, Judge?

BRACK I say that honour and reputation can be hugely attractive things.

TESMAN Of course they can, but –

HEDDA Gentlemen. Would you care to have a drink?

BRACK One before we go. That can't be a bad thing.

TESMAN Wonderful, Hedda. Quite wonderful. This is turning out to be an excellent evening.

HEDDA Please, you too, Mr Lovborg.

LOVBORG Thank you very much. But not for me.

BRACK Good God, one glass is surely harmless?

LOVBORG Not to everyone.

HEDDA Fine then. I suppose I can entertain Mr Lovborg for a while.

TESMAN Thank you, my dear.

> **BRACK** *and* **TESMAN** *go to the back room.* **HEDDA** *and* **LOVBORG** *stay in the front room.*

HEDDA I can show you some photographs from our trip, if you like. We travelled through Tirol on our way back.

She takes out the album.

These mountains here, those are Ortlers. Tesman has noted it just there. See, it says: the Ortler Mountains near Meran.

LOVBORG Hedda. Gabler.

HEDDA Hush now.

LOVBORG Hedda Gabler.

HEDDA Yes. That was my name. At the time we knew each other.

LOVBORG So, I should try to lose the habit of calling you... Hedda Gabler?

HEDDA Yes, you should. And the sooner you stop, the better.

LOVBORG Hedda Gabler married. And married to Jorgen Tesman.

HEDDA As it happens.

LOVBORG Hedda. How could you waste yourself like that?

HEDDA Now. None of that please.

LOVBORG None of what?

TESMAN comes in.

HEDDA And this Mr Lovborg, this was taken in Ampezzo Valley. Just look at those peaks. What were they called, darling?

TESMAN Let me see. Dolomites, that's it.

HEDDA Of course. These are the Dolomites, Mr Lovborg.

LOVBORG Are they?

TESMAN I was wondering, should I not bring you a glass after all. Even just for you, my dear?

HEDDA Yes, maybe. And maybe a few cakes as well.

TESMAN A cigarette?

HEDDA No.

TESMAN Fine.

He goes back to the back room.

LOVBORG So then. Are you going to tell me?

HEDDA Tell you what?

LOVBORG How could you waste yourself like that, Hedda?

HEDDA If you don't stop calling me Hedda, I will stop talking to you.

LOVBORG Not even when we are alone?

HEDDA No.

LOVBORG –

HEDDA You are allowed to think it. But not to say it.

LOVBORG I see. It offends your love for Jorgen Tesman.

HEDDA Love? Now that's a good one.

LOVBORG Not love then?

HEDDA Stop it. I will not allow any kind of disloyalty here. Absolutely not.

LOVBORG Tell me one thing, though...

TESMAN *enters.*

TESMAN Here we are. Here are the treats.

HEDDA Look now. You've filled both glasses. And Mr Lovborg is not / having any.

TESMAN It's for Mrs Elvsted. She'll be here soon.

HEDDA Mrs Elvsted, of course.

TESMAN Did you forget about her?

HEDDA We were so absorbed in this. Do you remember this village?

TESMAN The one below the Brenner Pass. Oh, we had that fantastic night –

HEDDA – with those wonderful guests.

TESMAN Of course I remember it. I wish you were there Eilert, it was extraordinary.

HEDDA *(re drinks)* Thank you, my dear.

TESMAN My pleasure.

TESMAN *leaves.*

LOVBORG Tell me just this one thing, Hedda.

HEDDA Go on then.

LOVBORG Was there no love in our relationship either? Not even a bit. A hint?

HEDDA I wonder if there was. I remember it more as a really close friendship. An intimate and honest friendship between two people.

You especially were very frank.

LOVBORG You encouraged it.

HEDDA I know. There was something so exciting, something daring in that kind of secret intimacy.

LOVBORG Yes. There was.

HEDDA In a friendship that no one else knew anything about.

LOVBORG I'd come to your father's in the afternoon, and the general would sit next to the window, reading papers. With his back to us –

HEDDA – and we'd be in the corner sofa –

LOVBORG – with a magazine in our hands.

HEDDA For the lack of albums.

LOVBORG And I confessed things to you. I told you things no one else knew about. I sat there admitting I'd been out drinking for days and nights. Drinking day after day.

HEDDA –

LOVBORG What power did you have to make me confess such things?

HEDDA You think I had power?

LOVBORG How else would you explain it?

HEDDA –

LOVBORG All those ambiguous questions you put to me –

HEDDA Which you understood perfectly well.

LOVBORG That you could sit there and ask those things. So boldly.

HEDDA "Ambiguously", please.

LOVBORG But so boldly as well. To ask me about all that.

HEDDA And for you to be ready to answer, Mr Lovborg.

LOVBORG Yes, that's the bit I don't really understand. Looking at it now, from a distance, was there love, underneath all that? Somewhere deep down?

HEDDA Was there?

LOVBORG Did you not want to find a way to cleanse me through my confessions? To make me pure.

HEDDA No. Not really.

LOVBORG What did you want then?

HEDDA Do you find it so unbelievable, that a young girl would simply like to know...

LOVBORG Yes?

HEDDA ...things she is not supposed to know? Just for herself. To get a glimpse into a life she is not supposed to see.

LOVBORG So that was it?

HEDDA Yes, that. As well.

LOVBORG Two allies desperate to experience everything life has to offer.

Why couldn't that continue?

HEDDA Well, that was your fault.

LOVBORG It was you who broke it off.

HEDDA Because we were on the verge of turning the relationship into something else. Something serious. You should be ashamed, Eilert Lovborg. You were going to take advantage of your ally.

LOVBORG Oh, why didn't you just finish the job? Why didn't you just shoot me, like you threatened to?

HEDDA Because of the scandal. That's how afraid I am of scandal.

LOVBORG So, really, you are a coward?

HEDDA Yes. Apparently, a terrible coward.

LOVBORG –

HEDDA But just as well for you. And now you have your Elvsteds to comfort you.

LOVBORG I know what Thea has confessed to you.

HEDDA And maybe you have confessed something to her as well. Something about us?

LOVBORG Not a word. And she's not smart enough to understand it.

HEDDA What do you mean"not smart enough"?

LOVBORG Not, when it comes to...those things.

HEDDA I am a coward. But I do have to confess something to you –

LOVBORG Go on.

HEDDA – not shooting you wasn't my most cowardly act that night.

LOVBORG Hedda Gabler.

And that right there, is why we were allies. You and I. Same desperation for the dangers of life...

HEDDA Careful now. Don't assume anything.

BERTE *comes in.* **MRS ELVSTED** *is with her.*

At last. Dear Thea. Come in, please.

I've been waiting for you.

MRS ELVSTED Should I go and say hello to your husband?

HEDDA Oh, not at all. They are leaving in a minute.

MRS ELVSTED Leaving?

HEDDA They are going to the party.

MRS ELVSTED *(to* **LOVBORG***)* But surely not you?

LOVBORG No.

HEDDA Mr Lovborg – is staying with us.

MRS ELVSTED Oh, it's so good to be here.

She is about to sit next to **LOVBORG**.

HEDDA Oh no, dear Thea. Why don't you sit here? Next to me.

MRS ELVSTED As you wish.

LOVBORG Oh, look at her. Isn't she lovely to look at?

HEDDA Just to look at?

LOVBORG Yes. She and I, we are true friends. We believe in each other – unconditionally. We talk to each other frankly and directly.

HEDDA No need for ambiguous questions then?

LOVBORG No, Mrs Tesman.

MRS ELVSTED Imagine, Hedda. He says I inspired him.

HEDDA He does, does he?

LOVBORG And how courageous she is to act the way she did, Mrs Tesman.

MRS ELVSTED Me, courageous?

LOVBORG Absolute courage when it comes to your friends.

HEDDA Courage. Yes. If only one had that.

MRS ELVSTED *(to* **LOVBORG***)* You are too kind.

HEDDA But now, dearest Thea, you must have a drink.

MRS ELVSTED No, thank you. I don't drink.

LOVBORG No, she doesn't drink.

HEDDA Well then you, Mr Lovborg.

LOVBORG Thank you, but neither do I.

MRS ELVSTED No, he doesn't either.

HEDDA But if I want you to?

LOVBORG It makes no difference to me.

HEDDA So I – poor thing – I haven't got even a tiny bit of power over you?

LOVBORG Not when it comes to this.

HEDDA Really now, I think you should have a glass. You know, for your own sake.

MRS ELVSTED But Hedda –

LOVBORG Why for my own sake?

HEDDA Or to be more precise, for everyone else's sake.

LOVBORG Why's that?

HEDDA Otherwise people might get an impression that you are not as bold, as manly as you should be.

MRS ELVSTED Hedda, no...

LOVBORG Well, people can believe whatever they want to believe. For now.

MRS ELVSTED That's right. They can.

HEDDA I saw it quite clearly in Judge Brack just now.

LOVBORG What did you see?

HEDDA The scorn in his smile when you didn't dare to join them.

LOVBORG Didn't dare? I simply preferred to stay here and talk to you.

MRS ELVSTED That was perfectly reasonable, Hedda.

HEDDA But the judge wouldn't know that, would he? I saw his face when you didn't have the guts to accept the invitation to their little party.

LOVBORG Are you saying I am a coward?

HEDDA Oh no, of course not. But Judge Brack might be thinking it. Or even saying it.

LOVBORG Well, let him.

HEDDA So you won't go with them?

LOVBORG I will stay here with you and Thea.

MRS ELVSTED Of course he will, Hedda.

HEDDA Congratulations. Holding fast to your principles. Just as a man should.

(*To* **THEA**) Isn't that exactly what I said this morning? You know, when you came to see us in such a panic.

LOVBORG Panic?

MRS ELVSTED Hedda. / Don't.

HEDDA Now you can see for yourself. No need to be so worried about him.

MRS ELVSTED Don't.

HEDDA Now that's resolved, we can have some fun.

LOVBORG What is going on, Mrs Tesman?

MRS ELVSTED Why?

LOVBORG Were you panicking? Because of me?

MRS ELVSTED (*to* **HEDDA**) Why /

LOVBORG So that was my friend's "unconditional trust" in me?

MRS ELVSTED Look, let me explain.

LOVBORG *takes one of the full glasses and raises it.*

LOVBORG To your good health, Thea.

MRS ELVSTED Don't...

He drinks it all, and takes the other one.

(*To* **HEDDA**) How could you want do this?

HEDDA "Want" to? Don't be absurd.

LOVBORG And to your health as well, Mrs Tesman. Thank you for the truth. Cheers!

LOVBORG *drains the glass and goes to fill it again,* HEDDA *stops him.*

HEDDA That's enough for now. Don't forget you are going to the party.

LOVBORG *fills another glass.*

LOVBORG Thea, be honest with me.

MRS ELVSTED Yes?

LOVBORG Does your husband know you came after me?

MRS ELVSTED No.

LOVBORG Did you and he agree for you to come to town and keep an eye on me? Did he put you up to this?

MRS ELVSTED No.

LOVBORG Did he want me back in the office? Did he miss me at the poker table?

MRS ELVSTED Of course not, Lovborg.

He lifts the glass again.

LOVBORG And to your husband's good health as well!

HEDDA No more now. You'll have to read from your book in a minute.

LOVBORG *puts his glass down. He takes a moment.*

LOVBORG I'm sorry, Thea. I made a fool out of myself. Forgive me, will you?

MRS ELVSTED –

LOVBORG I can still prove to you – to you and everyone else – I am reformed now.

MRS ELVSTED Thank you.

> **BRACK** *and* **TESMAN** *come in.*

BRACK Well, Mrs Tesman, the time has come.

HEDDA I imagine it has.

LOVBORG Mine too, Judge.

MRS ELVSTED Please, don't, Eilert.

LOVBORG Very kind of you to invite me.

BRACK So you are joining us after all.

LOVBORG Yes, thank you.

BRACK Excellent.

LOVBORG I would very much like to share a few paragraphs with you, before I submit it to the publishers.

TESMAN Now this will be fun! It's just... Hedda, how is Mrs Elvsted going to get home?

HEDDA Oh I'm sure we'll manage. Somehow.

LOVBORG I will come and fetch her, of course. Around ten, Mrs Tesman? Would that suit you?

MRS ELVSTED That / would be

HEDDA Yes, of course. That would suit just splendidly.

TESMAN Good. So everything is fine. But you mustn't expect me that early, Hedda.

HEDDA You stay as long as you like, my dear.

MRS ELVSTED In that case, Mr Lovborg, I will stay here until you come back.

LOVBORG Thank you, Mrs Elvsted.

BRACK Off we go then. There are "jolly" times to be had, as a certain beautiful lady would say it.

LOVBORG Around ten then.

BRACK So. Farewell ladies.

HEDDA Farewell.

BRACK, LOVBORG *and* **TESMAN** *exit.* **BERTE** *comes in.*

MRS ELVSTED What is this going to lead to?

HEDDA Oh, no need to worry. He'll be here at ten. I can see him. With vine leaves in his hair. Flushed and bold.

MRS ELVSTED I hope you are right.

HEDDA And then, you see, then he will know once and for all that he has regained control over himself. And he'll be a free man for the rest of his days.

MRS ELVSTED I pray it's the way you see it.

HEDDA Of course it is. You can doubt him as long as you wish, but I believe in him. And this will be his test.

MRS ELVSTED You are not doing this for him, are you?

HEDDA Of course not, Thea.

—

You can't imagine how poor I am, and how rich you are allowed to be.

HEDDA *looks at* **MRS ELVSTED** *more closely.*

I think I'll set your hair on fire after all.

MRS ELVSTED Let go of me!

You scare me, Hedda.

BERTE *enters.*

BERTE The tea is ready in the dining room, madam.

HEDDA Excellent. We'll be right there.

MRS ELVSTED No. No. Thank you. I'd rather go home alone.

HEDDA Oh nonsense. You'll have some tea first, you silly creature. And then – at ten o clock – Eilert Lovborg will be here. With vine-leaves in his hair. You'll see.

She almost pulls **MRS ELVSTED** *with her to the dining room.*

ACT III

Dawn. **MRS ELVSTED** *is wrapped up in a shawl.* **BERTE**
comes in with a letter.

MRS ELVSTED Was that someone at the door?

BERTE Just a letter.

MRS ELVSTED I'll take it.

BERTE Actually, madam, it's for the doctor.

MRS ELVSTED Is it?

BERTE Mrs Tesman's maid brought it in.

MRS ELVSTED You / should give it to.

BERTE I'll just leave it here.

MRS ELVSTED Nothing else?

BERTE No.

MRS ELVSTED I see.

BERTE –

MRS ELVSTED What?

BERTE I knew this was not going to end well.

MRS ELVSTED Did you?

BERTE When I saw the certain gentleman back in town, and
going off to the party. We heard a lot about him in the past
year?

MRS ELVSTED Have you?

BERTE Yes, madam.

HEDDA *comes in. She just woke up.*

HEDDA What was that?

MRS ELVSTED Just the maid.

HEDDA What time is it, Thea?

MRS ELVSTED Just after seven.

HEDDA Berte?

BERTE Tea, madam?

HEDDA Yes, please. *(To* **THEA***)* When did Tesman come home?

MRS ELVSTED He's hasn't. Not yet.

HEDDA He's not home yet?

MRS ELVSTED No. No one's back yet.

HEDDA And we were up waiting until four in the morning.

MRS ELVSTED We were indeed.

HEDDA Why do we bother?

MRS ELVSTED Did you manage to get any sleep?

HEDDA Yes. I think I slept tolerably well. Didn't you?

MRS ELVSTED Not a wink.

HEDDA There's nothing to worry about. It's obvious what happened.

MRS ELVSTED Is it?

HEDDA Judge Brack's parties always go on for far too long.

MRS ELVSTED They certainly do.

HEDDA And Tesman didn't want to wake us up, by coming in that late.

BERTE *is back with tea.*

He probably didn't want to show his face in that condition either.

MRS ELVSTED But where would he go?

HEDDA He's gone to his aunt's to sleep it off. His old room is always ready for him.

MRS ELVSTED No. A letter just arrived. For him, from his aunt. There.

HEDDA Then he stayed at Judge Brack's. Him and Eilert. Reading into the night from his new book. With vine-leaves in his hair.

MRS ELVSTED You don't really believe that's what actually happens, do you?

HEDDA Oh don't be silly, Thea.

HEDDA *pours some tea for* THEA *as well.*

You look tired.

MRS ELVSTED I am, yes.

HEDDA Then you must do as I say. Go to my room and rest for a bit.

MRS ELVSTED No, thank you. I wouldn't be able to sleep anyway.

HEDDA Of course you will. You were up all night.

MRS ELVSTED But your husband will be back soon, and then / I'll need to find out what's happened to –

HEDDA I'll come and get you as soon as he's back.

MRS ELVSTED Do you promise, Hedda?

HEDDA I promise. Go on, have some rest.

MRS ELVSTED All right. Thank you. I'll try then.

MRS ELVSTED *leaves.* HEDDA *pours some tea for herself. All the flowers are still in the room.* TESMAN *is tiptoeing into the room.*

HEDDA Good morning.

TESMAN Hedda! What on earth...

HEDDA –

TESMAN What are you doing up so early?

HEDDA It is early, isn't it?

TESMAN I was sure you were still asleep.

HEDDA Keep your voice down. Mrs Elvsted is sleeping in my room.

TESMAN Was she going to stay the night?

HEDDA Well no one came to fetch her, did they?

TESMAN No, I suppose not.

> **HEDDA** *pours herself more tea.*

HEDDA So did you have a "jolly" time at Judge Brack's?

TESMAN Were you worried about me?

HEDDA No, I wasn't. I asked you if you had a 'jolly' time.

TESMAN I did, yes. Especially at the beginning. We were at least an hour early and Brack was busy with the preparations, so Eilert read to me.

HEDDA Go on.

TESMAN You can not imagine how important this book is going to be. It might be one of the most remarkable things ever written.

HEDDA That's not what I was asking.

TESMAN I have to confess something, Hedda. While he was reading it, something ugly came / over me...

HEDDA Something ugly?

TESMAN I sat there and envied Eilert that he could write something like that. Can you imagine that?

HEDDA Yes, I can.

TESMAN And to know that, with all his talent, his appetites are still...so destructive.

HEDDA Are they?

TESMAN Well, he just can't control his urges, can he?

HEDDA And how did that manifest itself?

TESMAN I suppose the right word for what happened would be – an orgy.

HEDDA An orgy?

TESMAN Yes.

HEDDA Did he have the vine-leaves in his hair?

TESMAN What? No. Why would he do that?

HEDDA Oh, nothing.

TESMAN But he did make a long speech in praise of a woman who inspired his work.

HEDDA Did he?

TESMAN That's how he put it.

HEDDA Did he mention any names?

TESMAN That, he did not. But it must be Mrs Elvsted, who else?

HEDDA And where is he now?

TESMAN I last saw him on the way back to town, a few of us were going back, but instead we agreed to take Eilert home. He was in no state to be wandering around.

HEDDA I imagine he wasn't.

TESMAN But here is the most interesting thing, it's heart-breaking actually.

HEDDA Yes?

TESMAN I'm almost ashamed to tell you this. For him, not for me.

HEDDA Try anyway.

TESMAN I was a few steps behind the group, and do you know what I found?

HEDDA How could I possibly know that?

TESMAN You can't tell anyone, Hedda. For Eilert's sake. Do you promise?

HEDDA I promise.

TESMAN I found this.

He takes the manuscript out of his coat.

HEDDA Is that the parcel he was carrying yesterday?

TESMAN His precious, irreplaceable manuscript. And he didn't even notice.

Isn't that sad, Hedda?

HEDDA Why didn't you just give it back?

TESMAN I didn't dare. Not in the condition he was in.

HEDDA Did you tell the others?

TESMAN Of course not. I wouldn't do that, for Eilert's sake.

HEDDA So nobody knows you have Eilert's manuscript?

TESMAN No. And nobody must find out either.

HEDDA Does he know it?

TESMAN I didn't get to talk to him. By the time I caught up with the group, he and few others had disappeared.

HEDDA They probably took him home.

TESMAN They must have.

HEDDA So where have you been since?

TESMAN One of Brack's guests invited everyone back to his, for some breakfast, and morning coffee.

HEDDA Did he?

TESMAN I'll just have a little rest, and then as soon as Eilert is awake and recovered, I will take this back to him.

HEDDA No, don't give it back. I mean, not yet. Let me read it first.

TESMAN I couldn't possibly. I don't dare.

HEDDA You don't dare?

TESMAN Just imagine how desperate he'll be when he wakes up and realises it's missing. That's the only copy, he told us himself.

HEDDA Can he not just write it again?

TESMAN No, I wouldn't say so. The inspiration, you see / is a really important factor in something like...

HEDDA Ah, yes. The inspiration. There's a letter for you.

TESMAN Really?

HEDDA It arrived this morning.

TESMAN From Aunty Julie.

TESMAN *reads it.*

Oh, no.

HEDDA What is it?

TESMAN Aunty Rina is close to death.

HEDDA Well, that was expected, wasn't it?

TESMAN She says, if I want to see her again, I better hurry.

I will run just now.

HEDDA You'll run, will you?

TESMAN Could I possibly convince you to come with me?

HEDDA Don't ask me that. I'm not going to look at illness and ugliness. At least let me be free of all things ugly, will you?

TESMAN Very well... I hope I'm not too late.

HEDDA Well, you better run then.

BERTE *comes in.*

BERTE Judge Brack is outside. He's asking if he may come in.

TESMAN At this time of day? I can't see him now.

HEDDA But I can. Just let him in.

BERTE *goes.*

The manuscript, Tesman...

TESMAN Yes, give it to me.

HEDDA I'll put it away for now.

She puts the manuscript in the drawer. **JUDGE BRACK** *comes in.*

An early bird, aren't you?

BRACK I am indeed. *(To* **TESMAN***)* Are you on your way out as well?

TESMAN I have to go and see my aunts. Aunty Rina is on her deathbed.

BRACK Oh, Lord, is she? Well, don't let me keep you.

TESMAN Yes. I must go. Goodbye. Goodbye.

TESMAN *leaves.*

HEDDA I hear it was more than "jolly" back at yours last night.

BRACK Indeed. So jolly I had not had a chance to change yet.

HEDDA You neither?

BRACK What did Tesman tell you about last night?

HEDDA Nothing very interesting. They went somewhere and drank coffee.

BRACK Yes, I heard about the breakfast party. I believe Eilert missed it though.

HEDDA Yes, they saw him home first.

BRACK Tesman as well?

HEDDA No, a couple of others, he said.

BRACK Jorgen Tesman is a trusting soul.

HEDDA Why do you say so? Is there something you are not telling me?

BRACK There might be.

HEDDA Well, let's sit down then. Have a cup of tea, and tell me all about it.

BRACK Thank you.

HEDDA Well then?

BRACK You see, I had a reason to follow some of my guests last night.

HEDDA And would Eilert Lovborg be one of them?

BRACK I must confess, he would.

HEDDA Go on.

BRACK Do you know how he and his group spent the rest of the night?

HEDDA Is it something too rude to tell a lady?

BRACK They found themselves at a particularly animated soiree.

HEDDA Of the "jolly" kind.

BRACK The jolliest of them all.

HEDDA Tell me more.

BRACK Lovborg was invited earlier in the evening, but being a reformed man, he declined.

HEDDA But then, eventually, he went all the same.

BRACK Yes, you see, Mrs Hedda, something came over him last night at my house...

HEDDA I heard he was inspired.

BRACK Overwhelmingly inspired.

HEDDA Was he?

BRACK And he must have changed his mind. One thing led to another, and they ended up at Mademoiselle Diana's salon.

HEDDA Mademoiselle Diana's?

BRACK It was her who gave the soiree. For a select group of friends and admirers.

HEDDA The redhead?

BRACK Exactly.

I'm sure you've heard of her.

HEDDA I have, yes.

BRACK Not that long ago Eilert was one of her keenest protectors.

HEDDA So what happened there?

BRACK Quite a lot from what I hear. It all started pretty friendly between the two of them, but it ended in a fist fight.

HEDDA Between her and Lovborg?

BRACK Yes. He accused her and her friends of robbing him. He claimed they took some of his possessions, including his wallet. Apparently, he exploded.

HEDDA And then?

BRACK Then there was a general kerfuffle, including both ladies and gentlemen.

Police had to intervene.

HEDDA Who called the police?

BRACK That we don't know. But it looks like Eilert resisted the arrest, klopped one of the constables on the ear and tore up his coat.

So they took him to the station.

HEDDA And how do you know all this?

BRACK I enquired at the police.

HEDDA So no vine-leaves in his hair, after all.

BRACK Vine-leaves, Mrs Hedda?

HEDDA Tell me Judge, how come you are so closely following what Eilert Lovborg is up to?

BRACK For a start, it could reflect badly on me, if the investigation shows he went there straight from my house.

HEDDA Will there be an investigation?

BRACK Of course there will. But, as a friend of the family I also wanted to make sure that you and Tesman are fully informed of his nocturnal adventures.

HEDDA And why is that, Judge Brack?

BRACK I have a strong suspicion he will try to use this house as his cover.

HEDDA Why would you think that?

BRACK I'm not blind, Mrs Hedda. And neither are you. That Mrs Elvsted, she is not here by accident.

HEDDA If there was anything going on between those two, there are other places where they could meet.

BRACK Not in this town. After this, no decent house will welcome Eilert Lovborg anymore.

HEDDA Are you saying that we shouldn't either?

BRACK You see, it would be more than embarrassing for me if another gentleman was allowed to roam free in this house.

HEDDA Is that so? Roam free?

BRACK If he, this excessive and unpredictable person, was to find his way into our triangle.

HEDDA Into our triangle?

BRACK Exactly. To me, that would be the same as becoming homeless.

HEDDA So either the only cock in the yard, or...

BRACK Or no cock at all.

HEDDA I see.

BRACK And I'll defend my position with any weapon I have at my disposal.

HEDDA You are a dangerous man, Judge Brack.

BRACK Do you think so?

HEDDA I do. And to tell you the truth, I'm relieved we are just friends, and you hold no power over me.

BRACK How true. If I did, I might be capable of...well, who knows what.

HEDDA Now, Judge Brack. That almost sounds like you are threatening me.

BRACK Far from it. I prefer when the triangle is fortified – voluntarily.

HEDDA I agree with you.

BRACK Well then. Now that I've told you what I came to tell you, I must be going. Goodbye, Mrs Hedda.

HEDDA Through the garden again?

BRACK It's quicker.

HEDDA The back way.

BRACK I have no objection to going the back way. It can be quite exciting.

HEDDA You mean, if there are guns involved?

BRACK Oh, one surely wouldn't shoot a tame barnyard cock. Would they?

HEDDA No, not when one hasn't got more than one.

He leaves. **HEDDA** *takes the manuscript out. She opens it.*

BERTE *is heard from the hall. She puts the manuscript back.*

EILERT LOVBORG *bursts in while arguing with* **BERTE** *about her letting him in.*

Now Mr Lovborg, it's rather late for you to come for Thea.

LOVBORG Or rather early for me to come to you.

Forgive me.

HEDDA How did you know she was still here?

LOVBORG They told me at her lodgings she never came home.

HEDDA And did they have any opinion of her behaviour?

LOVBORG I know. I'm dragging her down with me.

HEDDA Are you?

LOVBORG Tesman is not up yet, is he?

HEDDA No. I don't / think so.

LOVBORG When did he get home?

HEDDA Late. Very late in fact.

LOVBORG Did he tell you anything?

HEDDA He said there was "jolly" time had by all, back at Judge Brack's.

LOVBORG Nothing else?

HEDDA No, I don't think so. But then I was still half asleep...

MRS ELVSTED *comes in.*

MRS ELVSTED Oh Lovborg, finally.

LOVBORG Yes, finally. And too late.

MRS ELVSTED Why is it too late?

LOVBORG It's too late, Thea. As far as I'm concerned, it's all finished.

MRS ELVSTED Don't say that.

LOVBORG You'll agree with me, once you / hear what happened.

MRS ELVSTED I don't want to hear it.

HEDDA I will leave you alone. / To talk in private.

LOVBORG No. Stay. Please stay.

MRS ELVSTED I said I don't want to hear any of it.

LOVBORG It's nothing to do with the adventures of the night.

MRS ELVSTED What is it then?

LOVBORG It's to do with you and me. We need to part. To go our separate ways.

MRS ELVSTED Go our separate ways?

HEDDA I knew it.

LOVBORG Thea, I have no more use for you.

MRS ELVSTED What did you say?

LOVBORG I don't need you any more.

MRS ELVSTED You don't need me?

LOVBORG No.

MRS ELVSTED No. You are wrong. I will help you now, as I did before. And we will go on working together.

LOVBORG I don't plan on writing ever again.

THEA So what am I supposed to do with my life then?

LOVBORG You must try to live your life as if you had never known me.

THEA I can't do that.

LOVBORG You'll have to try. Go. / Go home now.

THEA / No. I'm staying where you are.

> THEA *sits down. The time stops.* HEDDA *comes closer to look at* THEA, *sitting stubbornly at the table, looking at* EILERT, *challenging him. He is looking at her, not knowing how to respond.*

> HEDDA *looks at them both, separately, then together. She sits down as well. The time goes back to normal.*

LOVBORG Thea?

MRS ELVSTED I won't let you get rid of me just like that. I want to be here. I want to be next to you when the book comes out.

HEDDA Ah, your book. Of course.

LOVBORG Ours, mine and Thea's. Because that's what it is.

THEA It certainly is. And that's why I have the right to be next to you when it comes out.

I want to see all the honour and respect you'll be showered with. And the joy, I want to experience some of that joy as well.

LOVBORG Thea. The book is never coming out.

HEDDA What?

THEA Why is it not coming out?

LOVBORG There is no book.

THEA Lovborg, what have you done with it?

HEDDA Yes, what happened?

THEA Where is it?

LOVBORG Oh Thea, please don't ask me about it –

THEA I have the right to know. Tell me.

LOVBORG Fine. Fine.

THEA Right now.

LOVBORG I tore it into a thousand pieces.

THEA No.

HEDDA But that's / not really –

LOVBORG Not true?

HEDDA Well, if you say so. It just sounded so incredible.

LOVBORG Still true.

THEA Tore his own work into pieces.

LOVBORG I have torn my life to pieces. So I might as well tear my work too.

THEA So, that's what you did last night.

LOVBORG Precisely. Tore it into a thousand pieces, and scattered them into the sea. In the clear cold water. Let them drift. Drift in the currents and the wind.

After a while they sink. Slowly. Deeply. Just like me, Thea.

THEA You destroying that book, to me it feels like killing a child.

LOVBORG And you are right, of course. It was like a killing a child.

THEA So how could you then? It was my child as well.

HEDDA A child.

LOVBORG *doesn't reply.*

THEA So that is that then. Fine. I'm going to go, Hedda.

HEDDA But you are staying in town?

THEA Oh, I don't know what I will do. At the moment all I see is darkness.

MRS ELVSTED *leaves.*

HEDDA Are you not going to see her home, Mr Lovborg?

LOVBORG I? In public? People shouldn't see her with me.

HEDDA Of course, I don't know what happened last night, but whatever it was, is it really so irreversible?

LOVBORG It's never just one night, I know that only too well.

The thing is, I don't want to live that kind of life again. Not anymore. She has killed that urge and courage in me.

HEDDA That sweet little fool has had her fingers in someone else's fate.

LOVBORG She has.

HEDDA So how could you be so cruel to her?

LOVBORG Oh, don't say it's cruel.

HEDDA To go and destroy something that has filled her mind for a long, long time? How is that not cruel?

LOVBORG I can tell you the truth, Hedda.

HEDDA The truth?

LOVBORG But first you have to promise me – Thea will never find out what I'm about to tell you.

HEDDA You have my word.

LOVBORG I wasn't telling the truth, just now, when I told her what happened. I lied.

HEDDA About the manuscript?

LOVBORG Yes. I haven't torn it to pieces. Or thrown it into the sea. Or watched it sink.

HEDDA So – where is it then?

LOVBORG I have destroyed it all the same. Completely and utterly.

HEDDA I don't understand.

LOVBORG Thea said it feels like killing a child. But to kill one's child, that's not the worst thing a parent can do.

HEDDA Is it not?

LOVBORG No. I wanted to spare Thea from the horrible truth.

HEDDA And what is that?

LOVBORG Imagine a man. After a drunken night. Stumbling home to his child's mother and saying: you see, darling, I've been all over the place last night, and I had the child with me, and then I just lost it. Simply lost it. Who knows where it is and whose hands might be all over him now.

HEDDA But let's not forget, this is just a book after all. Not an actual child.

LOVBORG Thea's soul is in that book.

HEDDA Yes, I imagine it is.

LOVBORG So you must also understand...this means that there is no future for Thea and I.

HEDDA So what do you do now?

LOVBORG Nothing. Finish this whole wretched business. The sooner, the better.

HEDDA Eilert Lovborg. Is there a way to finish it all beautifully?

LOVBORG Beautifully? As you used to say, with vine-leaves in the hair...

HEDDA Oh, no. I don't believe in vine-leaves any more. But there can still be beauty. For once.

LOVBORG –

HEDDA Goodbye.

LOVBORG –

HEDDA You must go now. And never come back again.

LOVBORG Yes. Right. Goodbye, Mrs Tesman. Give Tesman my regards.

> **LOVBORG** *is about to leave.*

HEDDA Wait. I have something for you. Something to remember me by.

HEDDA *goes to the drawer where the manuscript is. She pauses. She doesn't take the manuscript, she takes out the pistols and gives one to* **EILERT**.

LOVBORG Is this your gift?

HEDDA Do you remember it? It was pointed at you once.

LOVBORG You should have used it then.

HEDDA Well, here it is. You can use it now.

LOVBORG *takes the pistol.*

LOVBORG Thank you.

HEDDA Finish it beautifully. Promise me that, Eilert Lovborg. Do it beautifully.

LOVBORG Goodbye, Hedda Gabler.

HEDDA *listens at the door for a while. She goes to the desk and takes the manuscript out.*

She burns it. Page by page.

HEDDA Look. I'm burning your child, Thea.

Your and Lovborg's child. Look. It's gone. Gone forever.

ACT IV

Evening. **HEDDA** *is dressed in black.*

AUNT JULIE, *dressed in mourning, comes in.*

AUNT JULIE Well, here I am, Hedda. In black, yet again.

My poor sister, finally gone.

HEDDA I heard. Tesman sent a message.

AUNT JULIE Yes, he promised he would. But still. I felt that here – in the house of life – I need to bring the message of death myself.

HEDDA That's very kind of you.

AUNT JULIE If only our dear Rina hadn't departed just now. Hedda's house shouldn't carry grief at a time like this.

HEDDA But she died so peacefully, didn't she?

AUNT JULIE Yes. It was so peaceful, almost beautiful. And she was so happy to be able to see Jorgen once more. To say goodbye.

HEDDA Yes.

AUNT JULIE Has he not come home yet?

HEDDA No. He wrote saying not to expect him too soon.

Please, sit down.

AUNT JULIE I would love to, my dear, but I have very little time. I must attend to Rina, and prepare her as nicely as I can. She shall go to her grave looking beautiful.

HEDDA Isn't there anything I can help with?

AUNT JULIE Absolutely not. Hedda Tesman must not deal with such things.

HEDDA –

AUNT JULIE And she must not let her thoughts dwell on it either.

HEDDA Oh, one's thoughts. If only they could be controlled like that...

TESMAN *comes in.*

TESMAN Aunty Julie. I wasn't expecting to find you here.

HEDDA At last.

AUNT JULIE I was just leaving.

TESMAN Look, you and Hedda.

AUNT JULIE Did you do everything you promised you'll do?

TESMAN I forgot half of it, I'm afraid. I better come back to you in the morning. My head is so muddled, I can barely keep my thoughts together.

AUNT JULIE You mustn't think about it like that.

TESMAN I can't help it.

AUNT JULIE You should be happy in sorrow. Happy for what has happened. Just as I am.

TESMAN Of course, Aunty Rina.

HEDDA It will be lonely for you, Miss Tesman.

AUNT JULIE For a few days, yes. But I know it won't last. I'm sure Rina's little room won't be empty for too long.

TESMAN And who might be moving in?

AUNT JULIE There is always someone who needs looking after. Some poor soul that can't manage on their own.

HEDDA Will you really take on all that burden again?

AUNT JULIE A burden? Oh, bless you child – it has never been a burden for me.

HEDDA But if it's a stranger –

AUNT JULIE A sick person is never a stranger for too long. And I need someone to live for too. Although soon, you two might need an old aunty to help a little as well.

HEDDA You don't need to worry yourself about that.

TESMAN Just imagine, how lovely that would be?

HEDDA What would be?

TESMAN Never mind.

AUNT JULIE Well, I see you two have things to talk about. Hedda might have something to tell you.

HEDDA –

AUNT JULIE Goodbye now. I must get back home to Rina.

She pauses at the door.

How strange to think that she is both with my dear brother and with me at the same time.

TESMAN It is, isn't it.

AUNT JULIE *leaves.*

HEDDA That is interesting.

TESMAN What is?

HEDDA Aunt Rina's death seems to have affected you more than it did your aunt.

TESMAN Oh, it's not just Aunt Rina. It's Eilert that I am so worried about.

HEDDA Any news on him?

TESMAN I went to see him this afternoon, to tell him that his manuscript is safe and sound.

HEDDA And?

TESMAN He wasn't at home. But I saw Mrs Elvsted and she told me he was here earlier this morning.

HEDDA Yes. Just after you left.

TESMAN And apparently he said he's destroyed the manuscript?

HEDDA Yes, that's what he claimed.

TESMAN Good God. He must be losing his mind. Obviously, you didn't dare give him the manuscript while he was in that state.

HEDDA No, he doesn't have it.

TESMAN But you told him you have it?

HEDDA No. Did you mention it to Mrs Elvsted?

TESMAN No. But you should have told him. What if he gets desperate, if he tries to harm himself in some way? Let me have it, I'll take it to him just now.

HEDDA –

TESMAN Where is it?

HEDDA I don't have it any more.

TESMAN What do you mean you 'don't have it any more'?

HEDDA I've burned it – all of it.

TESMAN Burned! Burned Eilert's manuscript?

HEDDA Don't shout. Berte will hear you.

TESMAN Burnt it! But that's impossible.

HEDDA Well, it still happened.

TESMAN Do you realise what you have done? That's a crime, you can't just destroy someone else's property. Just ask Judge Brack, he'll confirm it.

HEDDA It may be advisable for you not to mention it – to Judge Brack or anyone else for that matter.

TESMAN How could you just go off and do something like that? How did that even cross your mind? Where did that come from?

HEDDA –

TESMAN Tell me!

HEDDA I did it for you, Tesman.

TESMAN For me?

HEDDA When you came home this morning and told me he read to you –

TESMAN What about it?

HEDDA You told me you were jealous of him and his work.

TESMAN Oh Lord, I didn't mean it so literally.

HEDDA Still. I couldn't bear the thought that someone else would overshadow you.

TESMAN Is that true?

HEDDA *nods.*

I never knew this, Hedda. I didn't know you loved me, like that.

HEDDA Well, then I might as well tell you...

TESMAN –

HEDDA Actually, better ask your aunt. She will tell you everything.

TESMAN I think I know. I know what you are trying to tell me.

HEDDA –

TESMAN Really? Has it really happened!

HEDDA Don't shout. Berte will hear you.

TESMAN Don't be silly. It's just Berte. I'll go and tell her myself.

HEDDA This will be the end of me. The end of me.

TESMAN What are you saying?

HEDDA All this – the whole charade, Jorgen.

TESMAN A charade? That I am so insanely happy?

HEDDA Yes.

TESMAN Perhaps I better not say anything to Berte.

–

But we must tell Aunty Julie.

TESMAN *smiles.*

HEDDA What?

TESMAN And you've started calling me Jorgen. Aunty Julie will be so happy. So happy.

HEDDA When she hears I burned Eilert's book?

TESMAN No, no one must find out what happened to the manuscript. But that you love me so much that you would do that for me, Hedda. Aunty Julie will certainly hear about that.

THEA *arrives.*

THEA Dear Hedda, I hope you don't mind me coming again?

HEDDA What happened, Thea?

THEA It's Eilert Lovborg. I am scared something awful has happened to him.

TESMAN What would make you think that, dear Mrs Elvsted?

THEA I heard them talking at my guest house. The most horrible rumours are going about town.

TESMAN Yes, I've heard something as well. But then I can testify he went straight to bed this morning.

HEDDA So – what did they say at the guest house?

THEA They mentioned the hospital –

TESMAN The hospital?

HEDDA Impossible.

THEA I was so scared for him. I went up to his lodgings and asked after him there.

HEDDA On your own? How could you do that?

THEA What else was I supposed to do? I couldn't bear not knowing.

TESMAN But he wasn't there?

THEA No. And they didn't know where he might be. They said he hadn't been home since yesterday afternoon.

TESMAN Yesterday. How strange.

THEA Oh God, I'm certain something horrible has happened to him!

TESMAN Hedda, dear. Suppose I went into town, and enquired in a few places –

HEDDA No, no, no. You stay out of that.

BERTE *lets* **JUDGE BRACK** *in.*

TESMAN Dear Judge. We weren't expecting you just now.

BRACK Yes. I had to come and see you.

TESMAN I see you've had the message from Aunty Julie.

BRACK Yes, I have heard of that too.

TESMAN Isn't it just sad?

BRACK Well, my dear Tesman, it depends how you look at it.

HEDDA Has something else happened?

BRACK It has, indeed.

THEA Is it Eilert Lovborg?

BRACK How did you know, Mrs Elvsted? Do you perhaps already know something...

THEA No, not at all. But / I had a feeling...

TESMAN Oh for God's sake, just say it already.

BRACK Well, regrettably, Eilert Lovborg has been taken to hospital. He was barely alive.

THEA Oh God, oh God –

TESMAN At the hospital. Barely alive?

HEDDA So quickly...

THEA The last time I saw him we argued, Hedda!

HEDDA But, Thea, Thea –

THEA I must go to him. While he is still alive!

BRACK No, that's impossible. No one is allowed to see him.

THEA Tell me, what happened. What was it?

TESMAN Surely he wouldn't harm himself, would he?

HEDDA I'm certain he has.

TESMAN Hedda, how can you / say such a thing.

BRACK In fact, you are right, Mrs Tesman.

THEA Oh, how terrible.

TESMAN So he did it himself? Who would have thought?

HEDDA He shot himself.

BRACK And again, you guess correctly, Mrs Tesman.

THEA When did it happen?

BRACK This afternoon. Between three and four.

TESMAN My dear God, so where did he do it?

BRACK Where?

TESMAN Yes.

BRACK Well, probably in his lodgings.

THEA That can't be right. I was there between six and seven.

BRACK Well then somewhere else. I don't know exactly. I just know that he was found – that he shot himself...through the chest.

THEA How... That he should end like that.

HEDDA Was it really through the chest?

BRACK Yes.

HEDDA So not through the temple?

BRACK Through the chest, Mrs Tesman.

HEDDA Well, yes. The chest will do.

BRACK What do you mean, Mrs Tesman?

HEDDA Oh, nothing. Don't mind me.

TESMAN And you say, there is no hope?

BRACK The wound is fatal. He is probably gone by now.

THEA I knew it. I knew it. It's all over now. Oh Hedda –

TESMAN But tell me, how did you get to know all this?

BRACK I have a friend at the police. An acquaintance who can keep me informed.

HEDDA At least he has done it.

TESMAN For God's sake what are you saying Hedda.

HEDDA I am saying that there is beauty in this.

BRACK But, Mrs Tesman –

TESMAN Beauty? No.

THEA Hedda, how can you talk about beauty when something like this has happened?

HEDDA Eilert Lovborg has settled his account with himself. He's had the courage to do what had to be done.

THEA I won't believe that for a second. No. What he has done, he has done in distraction.

TESMAN He has done it in despair.

HEDDA No. That he has not. I am certain of that.

THEA He has. In distraction. Just like when he destroyed his manuscript, tore it into pieces.

BRACK Is that what he has done?

BRACK Hmm. That is interesting.

TESMAN To think that Eilert would leave this world in such a way. And not to have left behind the one thing that would have established his name...maybe forever.

THEA If only it could be put together again.

TESMAN That would be remarkable. Imagine if we could. I would give anything / to be able to

THEA What if we could, Mr Tesman?

TESMAN What do you mean?

THEA *(takes pieces of paper from her coat)* Here. I've kept all the loose notes he made when he dictated the book to me.

HEDDA Ah.

TESMAN You kept them?

THEA Yes, they are all here. I took them with me, when I left home, they've been sitting in my pocket...

TESMAN Oh, let me see.

THEA They are all mixed up. So completely out of order.

TESMAN Still. Imagine if we could put it all back together?

THEA –

TESMAN Perhaps if we helped each other / the two of us, maybe we could...

THEA Maybe. Let's at least try.

TESMAN I think it might work.

You must understand, Hedda. I owe it to his memory.

HEDDA Perhaps so.

TESMAN What do you say, my dear Mrs Elvsted?

THEA I will try the best I can.

TESMAN Where shall we sit?

TESMAN *and* **THEA** *look for a place to spread the papers. They find a place and start to work on it.*

HEDDA *and* **BRACK** *are on their own.*

HEDDA What a relief. Hearing the news about Eilert Lovborg.

BRACK Relief?

HEDDA Yes.

BRACK Well, for him, it must have been a relief –

HEDDA I mean for me. A relief to know that something so courageous can happen in the world. An act of beauty.

BRACK Oh, Hedda.

HEDDA I know what you are going to say. Don't. You know what I'm talking about.

BRACK Has Eilert Lovborg meant to you more than you were willing to admit? Or am I mistaken?

HEDDA I don't answer such questions. What I do know is that Eilert has had the courage to live his life the way he wanted.

And then he left us in this final, beautiful, courageous act. He was brave enough to end his life under his own conditions.

BRACK It pains me, Mrs Hedda, but I am forced to tear you away from this beautiful make-believe.

HEDDA A make-believe?

BRACK You would find out anyway.

HEDDA What are you talking about?

BRACK He hasn't shot himself on purpose.

HEDDA Not on purpose?

BRACK No, the case of Eilert Lovborg, is not quite as I told it.

HEDDA Have you kept something back?

BRACK Yes.

HEDDA What?

BRACK For the sake of poor Mrs Elvsted, I have somewhat re-written the incident.

HEDDA Which parts?

BRACK For a start, the part about him still being alive. He is not.

HEDDA He died in the hospital?

BRACK Yes. Without regaining consciousness.

HEDDA What else?

BRACK That the event happened in his room.

HEDDA What difference does it make?

BRACK Some. Eilert Lovborg was found in madame Diana's boudoir.

HEDDA Impossible! He wouldn't have gone back there.

BRACK He was there just this afternoon. He came to claim something he said they stole from him. He was rambling about a child he has lost –

HEDDA I see.

BRACK He was found at the boudoir. With a pistol in his pocket. The shot was fatal.

HEDDA Shot in the chest –

BRACK Well, no.

HEDDA No?

BRACK In fact, the bullet went more into the...groin area.

HEDDA Not even that?

BRACK –

HEDDA Why? Why does everything I touch turn into something vile and ridiculous. Like a curse –

BRACK There is something else, Mrs Hedda.

HEDDA What is that?

BRACK The pistol he had on him / when he was found–

HEDDA What about it?

BRACK I think he stole it.

HEDDA Stole it? No. He wouldn't do such thing.

BRACK Anything else is impossible. He must have stolen it...

TESMAN and **THEA** *come in.*

TESMAN Hedda, I can't see a thing under that lamp.

HEDDA Yes, it must be hard.

TESMAN Would you mind terribly if we sat there for a little while?

HEDDA Of course.

No. Wait. Let me tidy first.

TESMAN Oh, no need to do that. There is plenty of room.

HEDDA Just let me do it.

She takes something out of the drawer.

TESMAN *puts the notes on the table. He and* **MRS ELVSTED** *sit down and start working again.*

HEDDA *comes back.*

Now sweet Thea. How is Eilert's memorial coming on?

THEA It won't be easy piecing it all together.

TESMAN But it will work. It has to.

HEDDA Well, there / might be–

TESMAN That's what I'm really good at – organising other people's work. Of course it will work.

HEDDA What was it you said about the pistol?

BRACK I said, he must have stolen it.

HEDDA Why do you say so?

BRACK Any other explanation would be just too improbable.

HEDDA How come?

BRACK Eilert Lovborg was here this morning. Is it not so?

HEDDA Yes. He was.

BRACK And you were alone with him?

HEDDA Yes. For a few moments.

BRACK And you didn't leave the room while he was here?

HEDDA No.

BRACK You might want to think about that again.

HEDDA But / I never–

BRACK Were you not out at all, even just for a moment?

HEDDA Yes, perhaps just for a moment. I might have gone out into the hall.

BRACK And where was the pistol case at the time?

HEDDA It was all the / way down–

BRACK Now, Mrs Hedda?

HEDDA It was right here. On the table.

BRACK And have you looked at them since. Have you checked that both pistols are still in there?

HEDDA No.

BRACK No need to. I saw the pistol Lovborg had on him, and I recognised it at once. Well, I saw it just yesterday.

HEDDA Have you, perhaps, got it with you?

BRACK No. The police / have it.

HEDDA What will they do with it?

BRACK They will try to find the owner.

HEDDA And do you think they will find them?

BRACK No, Hedda Gabler.

Not as long as I keep quiet.

HEDDA And if you don't keep quiet? What then?

BRACK There's always the story about him being a thief.

HEDDA I'd rather die.

BRACK One says such things, but one doesn't mean them.

HEDDA And if the pistol was not stolen. And the owner is found. What then?

BRACK Well then, Hedda – then we have a scandal.

HEDDA No!

BRACK Oh yes, and what a scandal. You would of course be called to the court. Both you and Mademoiselle Diana. She would obviously have to go into a detail of how it all fits together. Was it an accident or maybe a murder? Was he trying to pull the pistol out of his pocket and threaten her? And then it went off? Or has she snatched the pistol out of his hand, shot him, and then put the pistol back into his pocket? Now that sounds like something she would do. She is a hefty young woman, that lady Diana, isn't she?

HEDDA –

BRACK And all that would have to be discussed. Publicly.

HEDDA But all those affairs have nothing to do with me.

BRACK Maybe not, but you will be called to answer the question: why did you give Eilert Lovborg your pistol? And what are we to conclude from the fact that you gave it to him?

HEDDA –

BRACK Well, fortunately, you are in no danger as long as I keep quiet.

HEDDA As long as you keep quiet?

BRACK Yes, my dear.

HEDDA So you own me, Judge Brack. You have complete power over my future.

BRACK My dearest Hedda. You must believe me, I would never abuse the position I have.

HEDDA You still own me. I am subject to your will. I am not free. Not free at all.

BRACK One usually just puts up with the inevitable.

HEDDA Yes, one usually does.

She goes to TESMAN *and* THEA.

So, my darling. Is it working?

TESMAN God knows, my dear. It will take, at least, several months, possibly years.

HEDDA Of course it will.

She touches THEA's *hair.*

How does it feel, Thea? Sitting here, with my husband, just as you sat with Eilert Lovborg before?

THEA Oh God, if only I could inspire him as well.

HEDDA No doubt he will be inspired. Given time.

TESMAN You know what, Hedda, you might actually be right. It does feel different.

HEDDA –

TESMAN But go on, go and sit with the Judge.

HEDDA There is nothing you two might need me for?

TESMAN Oh, nothing at all. Judge Brack, would you be so kind as to keep Hedda company?

BRACK It will be a pleasure.

HEDDA Thank you, but no. I'm tired.

I need a little break from – all this.

TESMAN Yes, excellent idea.

> **HEDDA** *goes to another room. She sings a song.*

THEA Oh, what is that?

TESMAN Hedda! Hedda! Please, no joyful songs tonight. Just think of Aunty Rina. And Eilert.

HEDDA And I'll think of Aunt Julie. I'll think of them all!

> **HEDDA** *stops the time so she can do whatever she wants to do without anyone telling her to stop. All the words and all the music that was in her finally comes out. At the start it sounds like a scream, at the end it sounds like a song. She breathes out. She turns back to the room and starts the time again.*

TESMAN I don't think it's good for her to see us two at this sad work.

THEA You might be right.

TESMAN I was thinking, Mrs Elvsted, why don't you move in with Aunty Julie, and I'll come to see you every evening. Then we can work there. What do you say?

THEA Yes, that's a wonderful idea.

HEDDA So how do you imagine I will be spending my evenings then?

TESMAN Oh, I'm sure Judge Brack will be more than happy to keep you company.

BRACK With pleasure. I'll be here every single evening, Mrs Tesman.

HEDDA Every single evening.

BRACK And we shall certainly have fun. Just you and I.

HEDDA Yes, you'd like that Judge, wouldn't you?

Being the only cock in the barnyard.

HEDDA *goes to the gun she took out of the drawer earlier and shoots herself.*

THEA *screams. They all stand up.* HEDDA *is dead on the ground. They are all staring at her.*

TESMAN She shot herself.

THEA Shot herself.

They are all too shocked to move. HEDDA *opens her eyes, slowly peels off her costume and stands up leaving it on the ground.*

She shoots the costume several times. Everyone is staring at her. She looks at them all. She smiles. She looks at us.

She takes the gun and leaves through the auditorium.

BRACK God help us. People don't do such things.

HEDDA *(almost out)* Oh, shut up.

HEDDA GABLER *leaves into the future.*

The End

PROPERTY LIST

Flowers (p1)
Cup of tea Tesman brings on (p2)
Berte leaves to fetch pot of tea (p3)
Berte brings in tea (p4)
Parcel – wrapped (p8)
Pair of old slippers (in parcel) (p8)
Bunch of flowers (separate from others from Thea) (p12)
Card on bunch of flowers (p12)
Berte brings more tea (p15)
Letter written by Tesman (p22)
Berte takes the letter from Tesman (p23)
General Gablers pistols (p28)
Pistols and bullets (p29)
Pistol box (p30)
Paperbacks carried by Tesman (p34)
Lovborg's manuscript/book (p41)
Photo album (p44)
Drinks from Tesman- 2 glasses and a bottle (p46)
Letter from Aunt Julie (p57)
Berte brings tea (p58)
Tesman has manuscript in his coat (p62)
Hedda puts manuscript in the drawer (p64)
Hedda takes the manuscript out of the drawer, and puts it back in (p69)
Hedda gives the pistol to Eilert (p75)
Hedda takes the manuscript out and burns it page by page (p75)
Manuscript notes from Thea's pocket (p85)
Hedda takes something out of the drawer (p88)
Tesman puts the manuscript notes on the table (p88)
Hedda goes to the gun (p93)
Hedda takes the gun offstage at the end (p93)

LIGHTING / SOUND

The two worlds – one of Hedda's real life and one of what she can see when the time stops – are different. One is more naturalistic, belonging to late 19th century and the other is contemporary, belonging to the time and place of the production.

The song Hedda sings at the end of the play can be chosen by the production/director.

rce UK Ltd.
UK
5220217
K00001B/138/P

9 780573 113857

THIS IS NOT THE END

Visit samuelfrench.
and discover th
theatre bool
on the in

A vast range o
Acting and theatre

samuelfrench.

samuelfren

samuel fren

Lightning S
Milton Keyr
UKOW05f
295043